Healing Life's Hurts

10 Steps to Healing God's Way

Sharon Nelson

Cover Photograph: Bertha A. Brooks Photography

www.facebook.com/berthabrooksphotography

Make up: Natalie Roye's Beauty Bar LLC

Hair: Tellie Johnson

Table of Contents

Acknowledgements

The completion of this book is a vision board dream come true. Habakkuk 2:2 (KJV) says, "And the LORD answered me, and said, Write the vision, and make it plain upon tables, that he may run that readeth it." This book is literally that scripture coming to life.

First, I must thank my Lord and Savior Jesus Christ. It was only God who provided the words, motivation, guidance, and answer to my prayers that made this body of work possible so all glory to Him who alone is the Christ!

Next, to my amazing husband, Darius Nelson, who is the wind beneath my wings. This book was started long before we started dating but he has supported me in every possible way. Thank you for encouraging me and believing in me and providing feedback, loving, and covering me in prayer daily. Your love for me gives me immeasurable strength and peace. Thank you for being my sexy man of God and for standing for righteousness, uncompromised. You are truly a man after God's own heart and no one else on this earth can wash me in the water of the Word the way you do. I am grateful God showed you me and you obeyed.

To my son, Ernest Charles Hickerson, who in part is the reason I am alive today. At my lowest point, it was our mutual love for each other that snatched me back from suicidal thoughts. Son, thank you for being the man of God that you are and thank you for being a great son. I am so godly proud of you and can't wait to see how God is going to show off in your life. Remain obedient to the word of God as you have been taught and watch God see your every dream come alive. I decree and declare greatness in your life in Jesus name. Love you forever and a day.

To my sisters, Arlene and Yvonne Durham. My rocks who have had my back from the womb. My love for you is indescribable and I am the most blessed woman on the planet because God placed me in between two amazing Proverbs 31 women in birthing order who have always and will always have my back and my front. You are both godly anointed and I am so honored to share life's journey with you both. My amazing sisters in love, Eleanor Nelson and Jacqueline Hall, and Dolores Nelson, your love for me is amazing and I love you all forever.

To my brothers, Edward and Daniel, your protection all of life allowed me to live a life of safety knowing that no one could touch me, or they would see your wrath. Thank you for loving your little sister and taking dad's final request on his death bed to look after us seriously. Your love has been amazing to me. I also want to give honorable mention to my brothers who have transitioned, David Carter, Wallace Carter, Aaron Carter, and Paul Carter, until we meet again on the other side, continue to rest in Jesus. Special shout out to my brother in love, Dwight Nelson. Thank you for your unfailing love.

To my spiritual, God-given community. My Jesus, I don't know where to start. My first spiritual parents Bishop (Dr.) S. Todd Townsend, Sr and Dr. Cleo Vilina Townsend, you were with me in the worst season of my life and you cried with me, prayed over me, spoke into me, ushered me into praying in my heavenly language, trusted me enough to ordain me an Elder in the Lord's church and had my back in spirit. No words will ever be able describe my unbreakable bond and love toward you. My spiritual mentor, Elder Carmen Austin, you provided guidance when I felt lost; encouragement when I didn't want to go on; ministry opportunities when I doubted my gift; and the prophesy that led me to being the married woman I am today. Apostle Gilbert Coleman, thank you for being my safe haven and providing a set place for my healing process. My time at Freedom Christian Bible Fellowship gave me just what I needed in my most desolate time. Your words of prophesy and your word of love spoken to me and over me actually sustained me until I healed. I limped into your church spiritually broken, but I walked out spiritually tall and ready for my next season in life. To my LOOKING OUT THE WINDOW CLUB (insider), the group of spiritual sisters who are my consistent and continual village that keeps me grounded, loved, secured and accepted. My LOOKING OUT THE WINDOW CLUB includes: Elder Bessie Evans, my Titus 2 representation of godly wisdom in the earth; Leslie Atley, my smartest spiritual sister friend who speaks words of wisdom and guidance and rebuke when necessary; Elder Carmen Austin thank you for your spiritual mentorship that kept me on task; Pastor Doris Griffin, my very first prayer partner and sister indeed. Your love and commitment to friendship has been a breath of fresh air in my life; and last but certainly in no way the least, my Peter, Dana Moore. Dana you were there for me in my worst season like no one else. On the worst day of that season (you know what it is) you would not leave me. You spent that whole day with me and made sure I was straight. I will never forget all that you have been in my life.

To my new and amazing spiritual parents, Bishop John W. and Pastor Isha Edmondson, where in the world do I even start. You always say give us 6 months and we will change your life forever. It did not take nearly that long for you both to impact my life in a major way. I love you both infinity times infinity. Your love for me is a consistent reminder of how much God loves me that HE would give me a second set of spiritual parents like you two. Dad, thank you for going above and beyond to speak into me and my husband. Your leadership is incredible. The example of who you are in the spirit is unmatched by many. Thank you for encouraging me, trusting me to lead your people in worship and for just being there no matter what. MOM!!! Pastor Isha Edmondson (my Dad's Victoria Secret Model). I became enamored by your beauty, anointing and grace from day one. I think I am your biggest fan outside of Dad. I just love you and your wisdom. Thank you both for not only accepting me as your daughter but for truly walking out real parenthood in my life and in Darius' life as well.

To Giselle Ogando, thank you for your editing expertise, guidance, PUSH (LOL) and support in this process. You are truly gifted for this ministry, and your "comma" game is strong! Love you so much.

Foreword

Out the gate, in her first book, "Healing Life's Hurts" (Ten Steps to Healing God's Way); Sharon Nelson writes with profound and caring insight. Her tone, her words, her stories all come together like a grand symphony ushering you to safe places for rich recovery from life's unbearable heartaches, meltdowns, disappointments, and failures.

Like a skilled surgeon, she pens her story focused on helping and healing you through your most difficult and traumatic times. Imparting "Godly wisdom and spiritual truths;" Sharon provokes us to confidence in God's loving and healing grace while unmasking both the benefits and the pitfalls of pain at work in our lives. Her personal testimony invites us to join her before the Lord on the threshing floor as a critical transformational space where being honest with oneself in the presence of God makes all the difference between healing forward or being stuck. There, Sharon testifies of her realization that the limitations of the flesh and the brevity of life became her personal tutors to usher her to and through the battle against darkness and spiritual wickedness in high places. Her personal insight and testimony illustrates both the necessity and benefits of our personal growth pains. Sharon illustrates our need to take responsibility for our personal actions and contributions to the problems in our lives. Just as the nurse gently applies the bandages following the surgical procedure, Sharon also applies God's gentle wisdom in calling us to repent...even when we are hurting.

Sharon argues that "Healing Life's Hurts" places a priority on forgiveness and forgetting as a divine prescription and essential medication to our soul's wounds. In order to heal well over time, we need to have "a high level of control over our flesh" which cannot happen in the absence of forgiveness and forgetting. This pattern and habit of forgiveness is fortified within as we cling to the promises of God, particularly while in recovery. For Sharon, the intentional pursuit of a "post-divorce relationship" required more than was reasonable. But clinging to God's promises encouraged her to trust that He would carry her when and where she could not carry herself. As you read on, you will see her healing and success emerge. You will be encouraged to walk out of your distresses into your destiny as one whose steps have been ordered by God for such a time as this. Sharon's ability to walk into new possibilities, a bright new future, a new marriage, new opportunities, ministry, and friends will inspire you to get up from being down and allow God to heal every one of your hurts. This book will move you to stand against the ways and wiles of the devil, nourish your spirit with God's word as a lifestyle, and be strong in His gracious plan for your life while being a blessing to others at the same time.

I am certain that Sharon's transition from the deepest points of despair to the heights of recovery and newness in life will prove an exceptional read for you, just as it was for me.

~Bishop (Dr.) S. Todd Townsend, Sr and Dr. Cleo Vilina Townsend, The Resurrection Center

Foreword

In "Healing Life's Hurts" (Ten Steps to Healing God's Way), Sharon has found an effective way to offer people healing and hope following the painful experience of divorce and her life getting turned upside down. She provides practical guidelines for anyone forced to handle the extremely difficult issues of life-altering tragedies. Scores of relevant illustrations and very practical, biblically based insights reinforce the guidelines they suggest. The wisdom nuggets scattered throughout this book and Sharon's continual self-reflection are excellent for anyone that finds themselves in hurtful life challenging situations. We highly recommend this step-by-step manual for healing to anyone who is looking for hope and guidance through the hurts of life.

~Bishop John & Pastor Isha Edmondson, Victory In Christ Christian Center.

Preface

As I began to think about my preface, this rap popped into my head which is the beginning of the theme song to the TV Show, The Fresh Prince of Bel Air:

"Now this is a story all about how my life got flipped turned upside down. I'd like to take a minute just sit right there I'll tell you how I became……..HEALED"

As I approach this subject, I could not help but share with you this rap that popped into my head because it made me laugh. The Bible says that laughter does good like a medicine (Proverbs 17:22) besides, I love to laugh!

If you've ever experienced heartache at an unbearable level, then you will be able to relate to my journey. If you have ever felt like there was no way you could move on or get through a particular storm, then you will be able to identify with my pain. Even if you are in the middle of your unbearable, paralyzing storm right now, I pray that the pages that follow will bring immediate healing to your soul.

Some years ago, I lost a job that I loved and had worked on for 18 years; my marriage fell apart after 20 years; I left a church ministry that I loved and served with all my heart; we were in bankruptcy; we had a 13-year-old son entering teen years AND my mother died all within about 8 months' time. All of this happened while I was in the middle of completing my Master's in Business Administration and, more importantly, trying to make it through Macro-Economics. Because God is faithful and HE is who HE said HE is and HE does what HE says will do, I managed to graduate with my MBA the following year.

I want to make this disclaimer right now. This book is not so much about the details of how my marriage fell apart, but it is about how God put my life back together. My ex-husband is an anointed man of God, extraordinary musician, and great father to our son. Our post-marriage friendship has been amazing, and we happily co-parent our adult son. So, please don't focus on the cause of the demise of my first marriage but instead, let's celebrate the God that healed my broken heart.

I, immediately, began seeking God and set out on a journey of healing, forgiveness, and restoration. What I learned about myself, my GOD and HIS word is incredible. I want to share my journey of healing with the world because I realize that there are thousands, if not millions, of men, women and children that have experienced life's hurts and are stuck in their pain unable to begin the healing process of moving on to the greater things that God has in store for them. I want to share some things that I did to help me deal with the pain, and at the same time, helped me to remain functional. Remember that life does not press the pause button for us to have our proverbial "meltdowns". I'm not saying that you should not have a moment when you cry and/or find HEALTHY releases for your anxiety and pain, but I am saying don't stay there. At some point we must realize that pain and suffering will stay as long as we let it. You must make a conscientious decision that you must move on.

Philippians 3:13-14 lets us know to forget those things that are behind and press on toward the mark of the prize of the high calling of God in Christ Jesus. Sometimes, it's extremely difficult to forget "those things" especially if we are seeking healing from a broken relationship, sexual, physical or emotional abuse. I believe that, when God puts two people together in marriage, He blesses them with a love that is supposed to last an eternity. In spite of that, marriages still fall apart. Due to the fact that one or both partners don't know how to continue loving within a marriage in a healthy state, the love that God gave becomes distorted and the enemy uses those negative feelings to create drama in the lives of God's people. Likewise, in abusive relationships, our ability to forgive is predicated upon our ability to take it to the Lord and honestly leave it there.

So, I'm saying to you, if that is your situation, let go and let God. It's an old cliché but I promise you, if you apply it, your healing process will begin. In broken relationships, we must learn to love but love apart. When I think about my first marriage and how it dissolved, I think about so many things that happened that were so unfair. Some things were my issues and some things were not but that doesn't matter because I had to learn to love apart. Loving apart means still loving the person, and caring about their well-being, but letting go of the relationship and moving on.

We all know that into each life some rain must fall. Matthew 5:45 says that it rains on the just and unjust. The bad news is that everyone in life has crosses to bear. If you have never had life's problems take your breath away, then keep living. The good news is that God is able to keep you from falling (Jude 24). Some of us go through life's storms because of mistakes we made or because we failed to listen to God or Godly counsel, while others go through storms in life for what would appear to be no reason at all, look at Job. Just remember that when we are hard-pressed on every side, we are not crushed; when we are perplexed, we are not in despair; when we are persecuted, we are not forsaken; and when we are cast down, we are not destroyed (2 Cor:

4:8-9). Be encouraged; this pain, hurt, embarrassment, frustration, and agony will not destroy you. You are more than a conqueror (Rom. 8:37). I stood on the promises of these scriptures in my darkest hours and found strength and encouragement to keep going. It all boils down to the fact that, no matter what, God's got our back. It doesn't matter how badly we hurt or how defeated we feel or how persecuted we have been, we are not just conquerors but MORE THAN conquerors. HALLELUJAH!!!!

As you journey with me though this book, I pray that I am able to impart Godly wisdom and spiritual truths. I pray that this book will be a way out of pain, out of brokenness, out of despair, out of hurt, out of unforgiveness, out of hatred and into wholeness, forgiveness, and freedom. God never meant for us to suffer but to be in good health even as our soul prospers (3 John 1:2). Whether you agree or disagree with what I have to say, everyone must know that God is always there waiting for us to turn to Him for direction, guidance, love, peace, joy, and happiness. God has healing in His wings (Malachi 4:2) but you must dwell in the secret place of the Most High (Psalms 91:1) in order to receive it. I know, personally, what it feels like to have your heart crushed and how good it feels to talk to someone who cares about what you are going through and is even able to give you Godly wisdom, but do not substitute that for your quiet time with God. Your friends and family and support network love you and are there for you and you need that, (God knows I did), but more than that you need to give GOD time. God has what you need to get through this trying time. Your friends and loved ones are good for you but only God can do what is required to mend your brokenness. Don't neglect God or fail to dedicate time to HIM. I promise you HE will speak to you and heal you if you let Him but, He will NOT chase you down to heal you. You must be a God chaser in your brokenness.

Journey with me through my process of being healed of life's heartaches and pain as I believe that it will draw you closer to our creator and allow you to experience just how very much God loves you. I'm sure we have heard the old cliché that nothing can happen to you that God does not allow. Sometimes, we have to learn to accept what God allows and trust Him to carry us through it. If God allowed it, HE is well able to bring you through it. Just as Daniel was convinced that God was well able to bring him out of the lion's den and the three Hebrew boys were convinced that God would deliver them out of the fiery furnace and just as Caleb was convinced that the children of Israel were well able to take the Promise Land, you must convince yourself that God is well able to deliver you.

Speaking only for myself, I can say that I had to abandon the flesh and walk in the spirit to allow God to do HIS work in me. The flesh is a natural state and we naturally resort to the flesh but nothing good ever happens there. Romans 7:18 (KJV) says that in this flesh dwelleth no good thing. Romans 8:6 (KJV) says, "for to be carnally minded is death; but to be spiritually minded is life and peace." Please choose life and peace. Being carnal and lashing out against those that hurt you only brings death (spiritually). I recently stumbled across that verse in the Bible, so make sure you learn God's word because lack of knowledge of God's word will keep you living a defeated life and you will never know God's truths and promises to cling to in times of desperate need. Please understand that God is not obligated to function in your ignorance. Read His word and understand what our biblical roadmap has to say about your situation and then, when you pray, pray His word back to HIM because HE is obligated to respond if you are obedient to His word.

Please know that wherever this life leads you and whatever pain you bear, you are not alone because thousands, if not millions of other people, have already overcome what you feel is unbearable. Know that you will conquer, you will survive, you will make it and you will be victorious. As Forest Gump said, "Life is like a box of chocolates, you never know what you are going to get." Trust God no matter what, trust God no matter how, trust God no matter when, trust God no matter where. One of my favorite scriptures (and there are many-LOL) says, "Trust in the Lord with all thine heart; and lean not unto thine own understanding. In all thy ways acknowledge him, and he will direct thy paths." (Proverbs 3:5-6 KJV). God is able and HE won't fail because there is nothing too hard for Him. If you believe that, just take a moment and give God a real quick praise!!!!

STEP ONE

Acknowledge and Identify the Hurt

"Woe is me for my hurt! My wound is severe. But I say, Truly this is an infirmity, and I must bear it." Jeremiah 10:19 NKJV

Pain has a way of masking itself in many ways. In my storm, the loss of my job came first. I remember trying to be real spiritual by saying "I trust God." Trusting God is always in order but at the same time I was also not dealing with the pain of losing a job that I really loved. I was excited on one hand because I received a wonderful severance package, which afforded me an opportunity to take several months off before finding another job. This was a welcomed break as I was, at the time, taking one of the most difficult courses in my graduate degree program and dealing with an aging mother who alternated residences between the psychiatric ward of the hospital and a nursing home. On the other hand, I wasn't dealing with the pain I felt behind losing the job. The pain of losing my job had more to do with the fact that I loved my job. I had been in property management for this portfolio of commercial office buildings in the Philadelphia Suburbs for well over 17 years and I loved what I was doing. I started out as a secretary at the development company that constructed these buildings and I learned so much, and the more I learned about commercial real estate the more I fell in love with it.

I worked hard and volunteered to do the jobs no one wanted because it gave me more well-rounded experience in understanding all facets of my field. As I mentioned, I started out as a secretary and by the time the 17 years with these properties came to an end, I was a Senior Property Manager with two property managers under me whom I trained. My pain of losing my job didn't have anything to do with the fear of not being able to pay bills because of lack of income but had everything to do with the fact that I lived and breathed Commercial Real Estate. I was all in when it came to my job and it was so much of who I was and so much of what I loved. I had invested so much into this job and was rewarded with multiple promotions. It wasn't until my first lady at the time, Dr. Cleo Townsend, told me to "take some time and grieve" that I realized I had masked the pain of losing my favorite job under the umbrella of severance pay and the freedom I suddenly experienced. It never dawned on me that I was actually hurting from losing my job. I was hurt mostly because of the fact that I loved my job but partially because I didn't get hired by the company purchasing my office portfolio due to the hiring manager's prejudice.

I am grateful that I had surrounded myself with Godly people who are able to discern things in the spiritual realm and look beyond the fictitious façade of what I was exhibiting. By surrounding myself with great people, it allowed them to not only speak to me but also afforded them the opportunity to speak into me. Those words permeated the very fiber of my being and, thankfully, helped me to take an introspective look at that hurt allowing me to deal with it. I really had no idea that I needed to deal with any pain as it related to losing my job. I honestly thought that it was all about the money and excitement of being paid to work and not actually having to do anything in return (severance pay). Gone unchallenged, I am afraid of what that subconscious pain would have produced years from now. If I were to offer any advice at this point, I would suggest and strongly recommend that you surround yourself with Godly people that will speak life to your spirit man while you experience your storm. They should be people you trust, people you know are walking with God, and people you know care about you enough that they are not afraid to tell you the truth no matter what. Then you should be very open to receive it. Sometimes, the enemy uses offense to keep us from growing and receiving. However, we cannot be so easily offended when we know that people are being honest with us. Even if we don't want to receive it, we have to know that the right person speaking into our lives are only doing it for our good and most times it is God using them to correct a behavior or take a complete self-examination of our circumstance in order to openly deal with it and not bury it. As I heard many people say, "you can't conquer what you won't confront".

During this time of freedom that God provided, I grieved the loss of this job and had healthy dialog with God about how my life was changing and the frustration I felt about the changes taking place in my life at that time. I am a very regimented person and I don't like major changes when I am happy with the status quo. You see, in addition to losing my job, my mother took ill and fell into a comma and my marriage was falling apart. Just as Jeremiah acknowledged in chapter 10 verse 19, I had to acknowledge that this was MY hurt and I had to bear it. The worst part was that, even though I was married, I had to bear it alone. I could not run away from my pain, I could not pray it away, I could not worship it away, but I had to bear it. Praying and worshipping helped, please understand that; but, when God decides it is time for us to go to the next level in Him (which I asked for) then we must go ***through*** the process and not ***around***, ***over*** or ***under*** the process.

There is no escaping the process and there are no shortcuts for the process. I read a book once called "What To Wear To The War" by Warren Wiersbe (1986) and one of the chapters in the book was titled "Short Cuts Take Too Long". It dealt with the fact that we elongate the process when we circumvent the path (take shortcuts) God mapped for us to take. So, instead of fighting it, I went through it alone. Not always willingly and not always without crying out to God to remove the thorn, but I went through it. I began learning how to endure hardship as a good soldier (2 Timothy 2:3). I had to go through it alone even though I did not understand (at the time) why God had taken away most of the people I had come to lean on. I once heard Pastor Donnie McClurkin say that God often causes us to experience trials and tribulations alone because when we come out of it with the victory, it has to be unmistakably God that gets the glory for bringing us through and no one else. God will not share His glory with any man so, if that means going through a trial alone so that we give no one the credit and glory but God, then that's the way it has to be.

Not long after losing my job, my mother passed away, I left my church to heal and my husband requested a divorce. The pain was phenomenal, almost to the point that I could not bear it. There were days in which I literally thought at great length about taking my life. I was angry! I was bitter! I was enraged! I felt hopeless! Yes me, Jesus-loving Sharon was at a point of feeling all these negative emotions. I had mostly bad days for quite a few months. It took me a minute to come to myself as the story goes of the Prodigal son. Once I remembered who I was, it was then that I began seeking God on a regular basis by way of the "Threshing Floor" that I had set up in my home office. The Threshing Floor was a place referred to in 2 Samuel 24:18-25, as the place King David purchased from Araunah to pray for the children of Israel against a plague. It was a place where David prayed to God and God answered his prayers. Significant also because the temple in Jerusalem was built at a location that was a former threshing floor location. It represents a place of prayer. I was encouraged by Dr. Juanita Bynum to set up a Threshing Floor in my home after attending a Morning Glory session at Bishop T. D. Jakes Mega Fest in Atlanta, GA in 2004. When I got home from that trip the first thing I did (even before unpacking my bags) was set up a threshing floor that was dedicated to my private time of devotion, worship, and prayer.

My Threshing Floor proved to be life-changing and life saving for me because I would spend hours, even nights on my face before the Lord seeking Him for answers to why I was experiencing so much hurt and pain. I was desperate for answers and I was desperate for some relief from my pain. During that season God began drawing me closer to Him which increased my anointing and propelled me into the next dimension in HIM. I barely noticed the change because, at this point, I wasn't active in ministry as I had stepped away to heal; however, whenever God afforded me an opportunity to minister again I felt a connection to His presence that was different than before the storm and difficult to articulate. Let me also say that, even though I lost my mother during this time, God has an amazing way of letting me feel her presence and most importantly feel her anointing flow through me every opportunity I get to minister. I thank God for that. I often tell people that when I have to preach or lead worship, I literally feel my mother pushing me in my back. It's hard to explain but it is the most amazing feeling to be able to feel my mother's love whenever I have opportunity to minister. I also believe it is God's way of making sure I don't run from ministry opportunities. I say that because my first inclination to ministry opportunities is to say, "No." The weighty responsibility to speak for God or the responsibility to get God's presence in the room is frightening for me. Then there is the added fear of feeling inadequate and (as previously stated) shamefully comparing myself to others.

I never wanted to be a preacher and I tried to dodge it for a very long time, but God knows exactly how to get a "yes" from you because He is Omniscient (all knowing God). You see, my mother was an ordained Pastor. She had the holy ghost and was not afraid to worship God loudly (that's where I get it from) and proudly whenever the spirit hit her. She was a preaching machine. Growing up, I didn't understand her bold worship because we grew up in a relatively modest Methodist Church. Well, that is to say, it was modest until the spirit hit my mother. No one could holler "HALLELUJAH" like her and I mean NO ONE. I remember being embarrassed at times because she would worship and not care who didn't like her worship. HOWEVER, I get it now. My mother had been through so much and she loved how God brought her through, so she was NEVER ashamed to worship Him.

What was key for me in getting to this level of healing was acknowledging the pain and being real with God about how to bear it and how to own it. I tried not to make the mistake that I had witnessed people make of blaming others. I did not want this trial to turn me into an embittered woman. I've seen it happen in others and wanted no part of it. I thank God for the experience of counseling countless women and even the experience of knowing countless women who were unable to move on from a divorce or hurtful situation that turned them bitter. I thank God because it showed me what I didn't want for my life. I wanted to acknowledge and identify the hurt so that God could heal me and make me whole. AND, more importantly, I believe, I wanted to acknowledge the part my actions played in it all. I eventually came to understand that my experience would help others get through similar situations. I knew I had to fight through the difficult times so that my victory would bless others. I knew that people were watching from afar and I wanted my process to be a testimony of the goodness of God and demonstrate how following God gets God results.

In order to acknowledge and identify my pain, I had to tap into the spiritual realm. Why? Because in this flesh dwelleth no good thing. In my flesh, I would have made a complete mess of my life. In my flesh, I would have committed suicide. In my flesh, I would have probably committed a crime. I could not find answers to my trials in the flesh. In the flesh, it made no sense that after 18 years on a job the owners would sell all my properties and the new owners not hire me. In the flesh, it made no sense that the woman who had been my rock for 40 years would die. In the flesh, it made no sense that the man I loved for 25 years (5 years dating; 20 years married) would walk away and never return. It was only when I mustered up the strength to tap into the spiritual realm that God began to make the crooked places straight. It was only when I tapped into the spiritual realm that God really began my healing process. It was only when I tapped into the spiritual realm that I began to understand that God was taking me to the next level in Him and that my experiences were simply growing pains. It was real spiritual warfare that could not be won in the flesh. Remember, we don't wrestle against flesh and blood but against spiritual wickedness in high places (Ephesians 6:12).

One of the benefits of acknowledged pain in our lives is that it allows us to identify the role we played in arriving at our present state. In some instances, we contribute to our trials and in other instances, it is a part of growing in the grace and knowledge of the Lord Jesus Christ. Whatever the reason, we must be real with ourselves and look introspectively at ourselves to learn from our experiences. This has got to be one of the most difficult things for us to do. We often love to play the victim and have people feel sorry for us or even take our side, but we must fight past that and deal with ourselves and our own issues. No one ever wants to admit or address the part they played in a situation but I'm telling you it is so necessary for your healing. Identifying your own stankness (is that a word? – LOL) and allowing God to correct your behaviors so that you don't carry current issues and character flaws into your next level. We often wonder why we deal with repeat issues but, most times, it's because we haven't confronted ourselves. Remember, you can't conquer what you won't confront.

Identifying your pain through acknowledging and taking ownership of your stuff is a vitally important step in arriving to your place of healing and wholeness. Don't be afraid to be honest with yourself because failing to do so will manifest itself years later into ugly, ungodly habits. You want to acknowledge and confront your pain because you want to allow God to heal you; to get the gunk out of your soul so that you can be whole again. You don't want to walk around hurting because as we all know, HURT PEOPLE HURT PEOPLE! Be honest with yourself and do your work so you can heal properly. Nothing worse than a broken bone that heals crooked! You will make it out, you will be whole again, your broken heart will heal but only if you do not give up, do not throw in the towel. Many of us do not have the luxury of throwing in the towel. However, if you have thrown in the towel, then let me tell you what my former spiritual father, Bishop S. Todd Townsend, Sr., would tell you, you must go get it. Go get it, pick it up, and keep going. Trust God! God has an awesome track record and is worthy of our trust. We will dig into trusting God later but know that there is nothing that happens to you that God can't handle.

Acknowledge and identify your hurt so that God can begin His work in you. Remember that hurt people, hurt people. We must deal with our pain and hurt so that God can remove it and replace it with healing. As stated earlier, God cannot heal what we refuse to acknowledge. Hurt and pain that is not acknowledged and identified turns into bitterness. Bitterness turns into illnesses that, left unchecked, can kill us. Please choose life today by acknowledging and identifying your hurt and allow God to heal you.

My former co-Pastor, Dr. Cleo V. Townsend recommended a book to me during the difficult season called "Deadly Emotions" by Don Colbert. Don Colbert is a doctor who believes in God. The book basically documents the fact that negative emotions such as hate, anger and unforgiveness, to name a few, when left unchecked literally can lead to death. The book proves that scientifically these emotions can ultimately be deadly. This is why it is imperative that hurt is acknowledged and identified.

Step Two

Forgive and Forget Forever

"For if you forgive men their trespasses, your heavenly Father will also forgive you But if you do not forgive men their trespasses, neither will your Father forgive your trespasses."
Matthew 6:14-15 NKJV

Whew! This one right here was most difficult for me. In the last chapter I dealt with wanting to feel justified in letting everyone know you are the victim. This was where I had to fight the enemy the hardest. When I sat down and went through my struggle and pain and realized that it was not wholly my own doing, it really caused my flesh to rise. I was angry and hate began to rise in my spirit. However, I had just enough God in me and just enough experience in my walk with God to remain in my word. One thing I have to say about the word of God is, if you read it (study to show thyself approved – 2 Tim 2:15) God will speak and correct your stinking thinking. The Bible clearly states that we must forgive others as God has forgiven us. The Lord's Prayer teaches us to forgive our trespasses as we forgive those who trespass against us. Jesus tells the parable of the master whose debts were forgiven but in turn he would NOT forgive the debt owed to him. (Matthew 18:21-35). The Bible does not specify forgiveness based on offense it just simply says forgive. Turn the other cheek. Matthew 18:22, Jesus instructs Peter that he should forgive seventy times seven. Please understand that we will be forgiven by God only to the extent that we are able to forgive others.

Luke 12:48 implies to whom much is given much is required. We sometimes want to receive much from God but oftentimes struggle to give what is required to get the much. People play the lottery because they want to be millionaires and not really work for it. There is a work required of you for your healing, but are you ready to do the work to receive your healing? Are you ready to make the decision to forgive? The requirement is to forgive the person or forget the place or situation that hurt you. I was able to ultimately forgive my ex-husband for walking out on me. I have no bitterness toward him and, because God is who HE is, today I have wonderful friendship with that person (to GOD be the glory!). I don't say that to brag or to appear self-righteous, I say that to show you that it was all about me trusting God to do a work in me and let you know that when you make the decision to forgive, God will show up and show off. God lives inside me so I was able to forgive that person because I trust God and, just like I want to be forgiven when I hurt people, I must forgive. Matthew 6:14-15 (NKJV) says, "For if you forgive men their trespasses, your heavenly Father will also forgive you. But if you do not forgive men their trespasses, neither will your Father forgive your trespasses." That passage does not require exegesis or further explanation. It's real simple and God did not stutter or mix words, He made it plain and easy to understand that forgiveness of others is necessary, if we want God to forgive us when we sin.

I, initially, felt the requirement to forgive to be so unfair (again wanting to be the victim). Our forgiveness by God is conditional upon our ability to forgive others no matter what they've done to us. So many times we feel justified in not forgiving because the offense against us was tremendously painful. Please know that this is a natural (flesh) response and will produce a natural result. The goal here is to subdue the flesh and seek after spiritual responses in order to obtain spiritual (Godly) results. So, despite the pain, God instructs us to forgive. What I find amazing is that forgiveness is not what you say, it's how you act toward the person that hurt you. On numerous occasions I've seen people whose family members were murdered forgive the person that took the life of their loved one; yet, most of us struggle to forgive someone who sat in our favorite seat in church. I think about how God forgives us daily when we mess up, but we won't forgive others when they offend us on far less than our offense to God.

We must annihilate the "victim" mentality and embrace forgiveness so that we release God's hand to do a work in us. Besides, Jesus gave the ultimate demonstration of forgiveness with these words spoken from the cross "Father forgive them for they know not what they do" (Luke 23:34). If Jesus could forgive those that sent Him to the cross to die; I think at a minimum we should consider forgiving those that hurt us. At least we get to live after our offense. Jesus died at the hands of those He forgave.

First, I charge, challenge, and admonish you to forgive your transgressor. I challenge you to forgive everyone that offends you. I challenge you to forgive, first, because God commands us to forgive and, second, because unforgiveness wreaks havoc on our health, spirit, and relationships. Because God commands us to forgive, failure to forgive means we are actually acting in disobedience to God's will, God's command, and God's word. Obedience to God's word was the driving factor in my ability to forgive my ex-husband. I loved God more than I hated my ex-husband (most days!). I was afraid that, one day, I would mess up and need God's forgiveness but be unable to receive it because I was harboring unforgiveness in my spirit. Obedience to God's word will align the concept of obedience in every area of your life. How can we expect our children to be obedient to us when we won't obey God's word? Paul says in 2 Corinthians 10:5-6 (KJV),

"Casting down imaginations, and every high thing that exalteth itself against the knowledge of God, and bringing into captivity every thought to the obedience of Christ; _And having in a readiness to revenge all disobedience, when your obedience is fulfilled._"

God is saying, when your obedience is complete, then all disobedience will be punished. Our job is to forgive; punishment is God's business not ours. The misconception of holding on to unforgiveness is that our unforgiveness punishes the other person. The only thing unforgiveness does is make us sick in the long run. Why would you not forgive and move on? In most cases, the person we refuse to forgive has moved on with their life. Meanwhile, back at the ranch, you are walking around stuck and harboring unforgiveness. There is a saying that goes: unforgiveness is like you drinking poison expecting the other person to die. The amazing thing I found out about being able to forgive is that God so honors our willingness and ability to forgive those that hurt us that He will quickly move us past that season and into our new season of healing and breakthrough. When we refuse to forgive, we not only disobey God but because of our disobedience we set a negative course of disobedience all around us. If you are a parent and dealing with unforgiveness, then don't be surprised when your children start acting crazy.

No matter how much you chastise them and pray and cry, you delay God restoring order and all because you won't forgive. Forgiveness is required in order to align our lives with God's word. When we are obedient, remember that the reward is that God promised to avenge or exact satisfaction for all disobedience. The ability to truly forgive and FORGET has so much to do with the amount of control we have over our flesh. My prayer for everyone reading this book is that they are able to maintain a high level of control over their flesh and forgive. While no one is perfect, the ability to control our flesh will save us from unnecessary trials, heartaches, and frustrations.

Secondly, I challenge you to forgive because of what unforgiveness does to our bodies. It is a scientific fact that emotions are directly connected to our physical bodies. For years, scientists were of the belief that emotions were in the mind only. However, research has proven differently. I am by no means a scientist (not even close) but I can read and comprehend. And, what I've learned is that, when our bodies experience extreme emotion over a long period of time, it has a negative effect on our health. It makes us sick and over the long haul can create diseases in us. As mentioned in the last chapter, I strongly recommend you read "Deadly Emotions" By Dr. Don Colbert. It is a great book and it really helped me understand that I didn't want to harbor any deadly emotions in my body, mind, soul or spirit. When I read this book, I came to realize that hatred, bitterness, and envy could utterly make you sick. This was motivating for me because I refused to give my ex-husband the satisfaction of seeing me go down because he left me. I wanted no part of that. I wanted to be healthy and live better for me! Additionally, I wanted to experience the peace of God that comes from forgiveness. What we fail to realize is that, even if we feel justified in hating someone, the wonderful, sweet peace that resides on the other side of forgiveness is delayed when we don't forgive. When we fail to forgive, we keep our hands on the situation and immobilize God's ability to fully operate in our lives. It's like a lifeguard trying to save someone that is drowning but that person won't stop trying to swim so the lifeguard can save them. Eventually, the lifeguard has to let go because they are still unsuccessfully fighting to save their own life EVEN AFTER help has arrived. But, if you are drowning and you realize that help has arrived so you stop fighting and relax, the lifeguard can pull you to safety. Just as it is in the natural, so it is in the spiritual. God can only bring you to a place of peace once you take your hands off and forgive. God can't heal you (save you) if you haven't forgiven (stop fighting). Give God something to work with and go ahead and forgive. Don't just forgive because you expect something in return from that person but fully and wholly forgive so you can continue to live a happy life.

In all honesty, no one wins when we fail to forgive. Another reason to forgive is that, in divorce, our children suffer greatly. When we don't forgive in the case of divorce, it becomes difficult to be able to separate our relationship with that spouse from the relationship the child has with the spouse. During divorce, it's totally separate, and a lot of women get it confused and all wrong. I say that because I did initially. I didn't want my son to see his father initially because I felt like this, 'if he didn't want me, then he didn't want his son.' That is absolutely the wrong thought process and not always the case. Thank God it was not the case in my situation. When we harbor unforgiveness, we are unable to see the delineation of the two relationships clearly. Unforgiveness causes us to use our children to hurt our spouse but in most cases it's only the child that hurts. Remember, hurt people, hurt people. Because you are hurting, your actions and your words often hurt other people without you even realizing it and that is why it is so critical to just go ahead and forgive.

Words spoken out of hurt often hurt others and, because we have become so immune to the unhealthy conversations, we don't realize we are destroying people with our words all because we are harboring unforgiveness. I recently ran into this statement on social media, "Never trust your tongue when your heart is bitter or broken. Hush until you're healed." What a powerful statement. The sad part about the bitterness of unforgiveness is that no one really wants to be around a bitter, negative person. They are the people I love from afar. My peace cost me too much to surround myself with bitter people who stink up my environment.

I am grateful to God that I was able to quickly forgive my ex-husband. When I say quickly, I mean within two years. I'm not saying that I didn't run the gamut of emotions that are normal because I absolutely did. You know the crazy thoughts that Satan tries to place in your spirit. Yes, I had them, but I wasn't interested in keeping them. They felt good for about 5 minutes until the Holy Spirit grabbed me around my throat and reminded who and whose I was. I am the righteousness of God. God called me to be righteous and not ratchet. Huge difference. I was trying badly not to have any dumb days as my Bishop John Edmondson says.

Let me pause here to tell you about the pivotal moment in my journey to forgiveness. It all started when I decided to get away on vacation. I was in a lot of pain over losing my mother, losing my marriage, and losing my job. In the midst of all the pain of this journey, I decided that I would go away to the Bahamas for a week. I packed my and my son's bags, grabbed my niece to keep my son company, and off to the Bahamas we went. My goal was to read, relax, rest and recuperate from the emotional trauma I was experiencing. I remember taking the following items: Bible (I stayed in my word during the time); journal (I journaled obsessively); and a book called "*Why Did This Happen to Me?* (Finding God's Strength Through Life's Hurts and Heartaches)" by Pastor Ray Pritchard. These three items were what God used to systematically heal my heart in 7 days in the Bahamas. I know that sounds unbelievable, but I promise you it is true. You see, I made the conscious decision that I wanted to forgive and be free from spilling hurt all over everyone I touched. Forgiveness is a decision! People often ask me, "how did you forgive him?" My answer is always, "I made the decision." I was just at a place in my emotional maturity and in my walk with God where I wasn't interested in hurting people just because I was hurt. I have experienced it in others and wanted no part of it.

So, once I arrived at the resort in the Bahamas I had planned to sleep until 12 noon every day and then chill on the beach. Notice I said "I planned" but God had a whole other plan. The Bible says in Isaiah 55:9 that His ways are higher than our ways and His thoughts are higher than our thoughts. DAY 1, God wakes me up at around 4:00am. If you know me intimately, then you know I AM NOT A MORNING PERSON AT ALL! This wasn't like an alarm clock waking you up where you hit the snooze and fall back asleep for 10 minutes. Not at all, I was wide awake, like seriously wide awake annoyed and frustrated. Like I said, I DO NOT DO MORNINGS, meaning I don't do mornings well. So, when God woke me up (because it had to be God at that hour trust me) I laid there and tried to comfortably fall back asleep. That didn't work so I started squeezing my eyes shut really tight and that didn't work (LOL). I imagined God was in heaven laughing very loudly at me at this point. Then, I laid there in defiance for another hour and finally I realized I better get my life together, throw on some clothes, and go to the beach. Even though I wasn't happy at that awful hour of the morning. At 5am, the first morning of my planned relaxing vacation, I found myself on the lawn chair on the beach with my Bible, my journal, and my book, ANGRY (real talk)! Don't judge me as I stand in my truth LOL! I was up very early that first day, and I had such great fellowship with God that the next six mornings God and I didn't wrestle when He woke me up. Shucks, by day three, I had taken my shower at night and had my clothes laid out.

What God did to my heart, my soul, my spirit, and my world in the next 7 days was nothing short of a miracle. God had taken all my tears and collected them in a bottle (Psalm 56:8); He healed my broken heart and bound up my wounds (Psalm 147:3); and left me with perfect peace (Isaiah 26:3). This was all because of the VERY early morning meetings with God that week in the Bahamas. Even though, begrudgingly, I started my early morning meetings with HIM, by the end of the week my mind was steadfast, and I trusted Him. God allowed me, my son, and my niece to have an amazing vacation filled with fun, laughter, adventure, and unforgettable memories and that was the bonus for my obedience.

It is difficult to put into words the feeling that came over me as God put the pieces of my broken heart back together. I felt revived, renewed, and restored. I believe that, because I ultimately made the choice to do the right thing and pursue forgiveness and healing, my reward was that He responded by quickly healing my heart. From a spiritual perspective, those were the best 7 days of my life. The number 7 is the number of completion because God did a complete work by creating the entire world in 6 days and resting on the 7th. Every morning after ministering to my spirit, God allowed me to watch His sun rise over crystal clear aqua blue water and white sand. There is something about meeting with God early in the morning by the water. God gave me the most breathtaking view of the sun every morning for 7 days. We departed the Bahamas (get this) on Resurrection Sunday. HA! Doesn't God do all things well. I arrived back in the states on Resurrection Sunday, completely resurrected from my pain, resurrected from the embarrassment of divorce, and resurrected from my lack of forgiveness and from everything that held me back from walking into my new season.

The next day I called my ex-husband and not only told him I forgave him, but I also asked for forgiveness for whatever role I played in his departure. It was a conversation between the two of us that was God-ordained, and it catapulted into an amazing post-marriage friendship. I thank God that our friendship is a shining example of how divorced couples in the Kingdom of God should relate. NO HATE! God is just awesome like that. I got healed and my son, Ernest, and niece, Breyiana had an amazing time on the island.

The benefits that I experienced from God because God had given me the ability to forgive, are indescribable. Did you peep that? ***God gave me strength*** to forgive, then rewarded me for forgiveness as if I did it in my own strength! Who wouldn't serve a God like this? I read an article at www.theodysseyonline.com, written by Leanna Ritter, entitled: **If you don't heal what hurt you; you will bleed on people who didn't cut you (Published 9/17/2018).** There is an older woman in my life whom I greatly admire who, like me, had gone through a divorce. Knowing my story in detail, she confided in me that, if she had forgiven her ex-husband as quickly as I forgave mine, she is sure she wouldn't be on half the medicines she takes. Let my testimony be a motivating factor for your journey to forgiveness. James 4:14 says that our life is a vapor. We do not know what will happen tomorrow. Our lives are a vapor that appears for a little while and then vanishes. Tomorrow is not promised to any of us, so it is best to go ahead and forgive right away. Don't become an unfortunate victim to unforgiveness. The trauma that ensues from unforgiveness is simply not worth it. God's desire is that we prosper and be in good health (3 John 1:2) and we can't live a prosperous, healthy life when we fail to forgive. Philippians 3:13-14 says that we are to forget those things that are behind and press toward the mark of the prize of the high calling of God in Christ Jesus. Forgiveness allows us to forget what happened in the past and walk toward the future God has planned for us. Unforgiveness is like walking through life backwards fully expecting to see where you are going. That just isn't possible. People who fail to forgive are actually walking through life but can't really see where they are going.

Forgiveness does not mean you won't hurt. Forgiveness does not mean you won't cry (many nights). It does mean you have enough respect for yourself to be able to let go and look toward the future. Our failure to forgive keeps us tied to the past. We cannot move into our future destiny in God if we are stuck in the past. This Christian journey is just that, a journey. Our journey can only become a journey when we travel. When we travel, we pass through places on a temporary basis; not a permanent one. We should never purchase a house when we were only meant to get a hotel room for a short stay. Allow the pain that we feel to be a city that we pass through on our Christian journey, but never stop there long enough to set up residence. Please do not allow your painful situations and circumstances to allow you to be stuck. Failure to forgive stunts growth and that unforgiveness takes up residence in our spirit in a space that God intended for love to occupy. God is love, so we must allow God to replace all the hurt, unforgiveness and bitterness that we have allowed into our lives with His love. The bottom line is forgiveness is necessary for healing to take place. We must forgive before we can walk in our healing. Forgiveness is a process and, though we might decide to forgive, we must walk through the process that takes us from the decision to forgive to the manifestation of healing. It is a faith move. In 2 Corinthians 5:7, Paul said "for we walk by faith and not by sight." We must walk in our healing by faith knowing that, though it might not feel great immediately, we are already healed in the spirit; so we just simply walk to it by faith. Not by sight, but by faith.

I admonish you to make the conscious decision to forgive. Don't hold on to the idea of how you were mistreated or wronged. Just trust God and forgive. TRUST GOD AND FORGIVE! When you make the decision to forgive, God will honor it and do amazing things in your life as a result of your obedience to His word. Like Malachi said, test God and see for yourself. The other side of forgiveness is a life of victory. Not a perfect life, but it's a life filled with the knowledge that you overcame and were victorious over the enemy's attempt to distract and hold you back from what God has for you. It doesn't matter how justified you feel to hold on to your bitterness. Yes, in some instances the other person was dead wrong but that doesn't mean you lose by forgiving, you actually win. No, it isn't fair what happened to you, but will you trust God enough, will you trust His word enough to forgive anyway? If so, you will experience the same manifested blessings that I experienced. When I was a child, we used to sing this song "it is no secret what God can do, what He's done for others He'll do for you...." If God did it for me, trust and believe He will do it for you. God loves you so much and He is simply waiting for you to forgive so He can show off in your life! It's a decision. Will you decide today to Forgive and Forget Forever?

STEP THREE

Stand on God's Promises

"Grace and peace be multiplied to you in the knowledge of God and of Jesus our Lord, as His divine power has given to us all things that pertain to life and godliness, through the knowledge of Him who called us by glory and virtue, by which have been given to us exceedingly great and precious promises."

2 Peter 1:2-4a NKJV

In this process of healing, we must trust God and believe in His promises. God's promises are yes and amen. God's promises are plentiful. Believe Him! Believe His word! Trust Him! The text above in 2 Peter states that God provides everything we need pertaining to life and godliness through us knowing him. Through our process of forgiving, we truly get to know God and His power at a deeper level. Forgiveness is the obedience plan of God which forces us to stand on His promises for us because He promised us things when we obey His word. Standing on God's promises is trusting that what God said in His Word He is faithful to perform. Here are a few things that we learn for sure when we fully believe that we are STANDING on His promises;

- It gives us strength and power to continue on the journey.

- It fights against our desire to give up.

- It lets us know just how much God loves us and just how much He has our back.

- It lets us know that there is a host of saints that have gone on before us (the cloud of witnesses – Hebrew 12:1) who are looking over the bannister of heaven cheering us on.

On this healing journey, the ability to stand on God's promises is critical to your survival. You will have days when giving up and walking away from doing your healing work will appear to be easier. I wrote this book to tell you that giving up is not an option for you. Standing on the promises of God will destroy the desire to give up but only if you believe and apply the promises to your process. God's promises will be a balm of healing to your soul if you stand on them.

I remember as a kid when my mother would promise me a reward in exchange for obedience to her instructions. I would be so motived to obey because I knew I could stand on her promise to bless me with whatever was promised. What I loved most was when she promised to take me clothes shopping. She could get me to do almost anything for a promised trip to Fashion Bug. Just like it is in the natural, it is in the spirit. When we obey God's word, we can fully expect Him to perform His word in our lives and our expectancy of His performance is how we stand on His promise. I submit to you today that you will not waste your effort of expectancy because God is not a man that He should lie (Numbers 23:19). If He said it in His word, then you can take it to the bank, baby! He is a true and honest gentleman who stands by what He promised. Try Him, test Him, you'll see. The word of God is full of examples of men and women of God who stood on God's promises and obeyed His word and experienced His blessing.

After I forgave my ex-husband and started out on this venture to develop and maintain this post-divorce relationship, I found myself trying to navigate through being single. I had never been single as an adult because I had been with him since the age of 16. Standing on God's promises, at this point of my life, was critical to my survival. Going from a two-income household to a one income household is a challenge in and of itself but, as I stated earlier, we were in bankruptcy so that added fuel to the financial fire. I had a resolve to stand on the promises like never before because God's word was literally the only thing keeping me from jumping off a bridge. Even though I had forgiven my ex-husband, I still had to battle depression and suicidal thoughts due to loneliness and the struggle of doing life by myself without a mate after a 20-year marriage. As I look back on those times, I can say that it was only God that brought me through. IT WAS RIGHT ALONG THROUGH HERE, WHERE THERE WAS ONLY ONE SET OF FOOTPRINTS IN THE SAND! If you don't understand the last sentence, then Google the poem "Footprints in The Sand."

The scriptures that follow are the promises of God that kept me during the most difficult time of my life. I am sharing them with you and declaring that you will find the same strength, hope, deliverance, fortitude, refuge, encouragement, and restoration of God that I found. These scriptures sustained me. There comes a time in your life when quoting scriptures is cute, but it isn't enough. You have to come to a place in your Christian journey that you walk it out and actually APPLY the word of God to your situation. You are either going to believe God's word, or you are not! I chose to believe and stand because I had no other choice but trust him or die.

Philippians 4:19 *KJV*

"But my God shall supply all your need according to his riches in glory by Christ Jesus."

I remember praying this scripture to God repeatedly during my wilderness experience. I remember saying, "now God you said you would supply…." Because at times things looked really bleak and I could barely afford to pay attention let alone all my bills and put food on the table and clothes on my and my son's back. However, I paid my tithes and stood on His word. God did exactly as He promised. All our needs were met because God is a perfect gentleman and He kept His word to me. Needs were not met the way I wanted them met all the time, but I promise you that every need I had was met. Like I said, God is a perfect gentleman in keeping His word. In order to effectively stand on God's promises, you must be open to His commitment to keep them however He chooses because His ways are so much better than ours. We just have to humble ourselves to receive it however God gives it. I remember bartering with my girlfriend Dana Moore. She was a great cook and I could braid little girl's hair extremely well. She had a daughter whose hair needed to be braided and I had a 13-year old growing boy who needed to eat. She fed us some days and I cornrowed her daughter's hair. Sometimes, you have to work the system and resources that God places in your life and never be ashamed to let your needs be known.

John 16:33 KJV

"These things I have spoken unto you, that in me ye might have peace. In the world ye shall have tribulation; but be of good cheer, I have overcome the world."

I don't believe anyone is exempt from trials and difficult seasons. We don't get to:

- choose **what** our "go through" will be

- choose **when** our "go through" will be

- choose **how** our "go through" will be

Wouldn't it be nice if we could choose? Since we cannot, then our only responsibility is to trust God's promises through it and know that He has us in the palm of his hand. God has already overcome; He has already obtained and secured our victory. We just have to keep living through it because after it comes the victory (in the words of Ricky Dillard). I found great comfort in knowing that even in my trial and tribulation God said I can have peace and I honestly did most days. Even though it didn't make sense and it wasn't fair, and I couldn't make ends meet at times, I had incredible peace that only God could provide. This text gave me such hope on my worst days. I just had to keep saying to my flesh, be of good cheer God has already won for you. It was difficult somedays, but I just kept quoting this scripture to my flesh so that my flesh and spirit would work together and fight this good fight of faith.

Isaiah 41:10 NKJV

"Fear not, for I am with you; Be not dismayed, for I am your God. I will strengthen you, Yes, I will help you, I will uphold you with My righteous right hand."

When God says He is with you, He really means it. God never left me during my difficult season. When strong feelings of loneliness would come upon me, I remember calling out to God with tears in my eyes and I literally felt Him **strengthening** me. God held me on days when I could not hold myself. As I mentioned in my preface, when life comes along and kicks you in the gut, there is no pause button for you to stop and have an adult temper tantrum or adult pity party. You have to keep living, especially if you have children. I remember having to get up and go to work after having cried all night long trying to find a way to get rid of the red eyes and swollen skin under my eyes. I felt like giving up; I felt like running away and never coming back, but God was upholding me with His righteous right hand. I could not give up, I could not throw in the towel, and I could not remain in a state of depression. I had to keep fighting because I had a teenage son whose life depended on me fighting back and winning. Besides, He needed to see God show up for me as a point of reference for how God would show up for him in his storms. Similar to how I saw my mom fight back and saw God show up for her. The first two words of this text remind me of one of my favorite preachers (I have many) Bishop Joseph Garlington. In one of his many sermons I repeatedly listened to in this season he said, "Always in the Bible when God says, 'fear not' it's already too late." LOL. Meaning the situation that is causing fear is already upon us. But I thank God that, when fear is upon us, we have the blessed peace to know that God will uphold us with His righteous right hand.

If you have walked with God for any amount of time, then you know that no one can hold you like God can. This scripture gave me life and hope and strength. It allowed me to keep living to the next day and the next day turned into the next month and the next month turned into the next year. Only God can move you through a difficult time like that but only when you stand on His promises. I remember being so afraid because I no longer had a man in the house with me. The enemy kept saying to me, "what are you going to do if someone tries to rob your house, you don't have a man to protect you." The devil is a foul tormenting spirit. I was so afraid, at times, but I had just enough word in me to quote back to him, "God has not given me a spirit of fear but of power, love and a sound mind" (2 Tim 1:7). One amazing verse that I loved to throw back in the devil's face whenever I felt fearful in the house without a man was "The LORD is on my side; I will not fear. What can man do to me?" (Psalm 118:6 ESV) You want to check mate the devil? Answer his stupid thoughts with a question. What can man do to me? HA! That shut him right up. Call me deep and extra spiritual but I went and got my blessed oil and anointed my door post and all the windows in my house and I never had that specific spirit of fear ever again. God gave me sweet rest in Him all because I had enough sense to trust Him and stand on His promises. Let me take a moment to encourage you to get into your word and read it. It's full of weapons to whip the devil's rotten tail. HA! I LUH GOD!!

1 Peter 5:7 KJV

"Casting all your cares on him; for he careth for you."

As I begin to meditate on the word more, and more, I got this Holy Ghost boldness/swag that I never had before. I got to a place where EVERY concern, EVERY care was placed on God. No matter how difficult it was, no matter how troubling it was, I literally felt like it was God's job to fix it. I would pray and quote this promise back to God and I can tell you that I stand here today because He is a keeper of His promises. Against all odds, God does care for you. In the middle of your battle, please know that God cares for you. You can really take your cares to the Lord and leave them there. He's got you. I know sometimes life gets very hard but there is a peace in knowing that God cares. We only need to remember to go to Him, to rely on Him, to trust in Him, and cast our cares.

It was difficult, at first, to remember to tap into the spiritual realm and cast my cares on Him because initially I was angry, and I wanted to fight back and lash out. This whole standing on the promises took some prayer and practice "chile"! Some days my flesh was just tripping. HOWEVER, after a while, I would laugh at the devil because my spiritual discernment would kick in and God began to show me the enemy's tricks and give me revelation that it was him. This only happened because I was determined to do this God's way and not lose by fighting in the natural. Even though the attacks didn't stop coming, they hit different when you know whose you are and how much HE cares.

2 Corinthians 4:8-9 *KJV*

"We are troubled on every side, yet not distressed; we are perplexed but not in despair; persecuted but not forsaken; cast down, but not destroyed."

Hear ye, hear ye, this text right here is the wind beneath my wings. To me it says, no matter what the devil throws at you, God has a catcher's mitt and is standing right in front of you catching everything the enemy tries to hurl at you. You may have trouble, but the trouble won't have you. You may feel the pain, but the pain won't kill you. You may be persecuted but you will not be forsaken because God is right there by your side. The weapons may form; and they don't feel good or look good, but they will not prosper (Isaiah 54:17). You must know that you know that you know that God has your back, your front, your sides, your top and your bottom in Jesus name. The enemy's tricks are just that, tricks. If you are my age, then you know tricks are for kids! Satan only wins when we fail to tap into the spirit. This is a spiritual fight that can only be fought in the spirit.

Fighting in the flesh means you will lose. Our fight is not with man but with the devil. Remember we wrestle not against flesh and blood (Ephesians 6:12) even though that's what is always in our face as Bishop Joseph Garlington once said. That enemy is a trickster but when you've drawn close to God and God has drawn close to you; the enemy's tactics don't work for long, if at all. Our spiritual fight is won when we are effectively standing on

God's promises. The word of God reminds us in 2 Chronicles 20 that, if we are inquiring of the Lord in this battle as Jehoshaphat did, then there are some fights that we won't even have to fight. I'm trying to operate in a way that not having to fight is my constant testimony. God will fight it for us and allow us to collect the enemy's spoils. The enemy is already defeated, and his only weapon is deception but once you are hip to his devices, then you can fight him and win.

Romans 8:18 KJV

"For I reckon that the sufferings of this present time are not worthy to be compared with the glory which shall be revealed in us."

Even though my heart was torn into what felt like a million pieces, this text right here gave me hope that, if I could just hold on a little while longer, everything would be alright. If I could just get through this period of suffering, it would get better later. Then knowing that the suffering would be nothing compared to the glory that God would reveal in me. Take the suffering, get God's glory! Got it! This is the promise that God gave us in HIS word that I was just crazy enough to believe. I held on to this text and I repeated it to God daily in my time with Him. I constantly reminded Him of His promises to me and I spoke life into my brokenness with His word. This was not always easy. Some days, I just laid in His presence and cried and that is okay to do because tears are cleansing for the soul. After you get up from crying though, STAND on the word of God.

When we stand on the word of God, we literally give God room to do a great and mighty work in us. Instead of focusing on our pain, we should focus on the promises God gave us to get us through the pain. There is another side to this pain and devastation that we will get to see and live and experience if we would just hold on and stand on God's promises. Sometimes, we can't control what happens to us. What we can control is strengthening our faith and strengthening our inner man (Ephesians 3:16) so that we can endure the hardship as a good soldier (2

Timothy 2:3). God's promises are plentiful, and they provide strength, endurance, and sustainability when the storms of life have taken our breath away. Get into God's word and learn His promises for you. It is His good pleasure to perform His word in your life when we stand on what He said. The word of God is full of goodness and, when we read it, study it, and apply it; we are strengthened and encouraged and renewed and restored. It is all good stuff, but we need to open the book. It was literally my survivors guide to living life abundantly.

Ecclesiastes 7:8 KJV

"Better is the end of a thing than the beginning thereof: and the patient in spirit is better than the proud spirit."

I remember screaming this promise to God OFTEN. I would get excited when I read this text because it promised me that things would get better than they were at that moment. I looked forward to the end of my hurt, the end of my storm, the end of my trial, and the end of my test. God promised that it would get better and it did, just as He said. This was the text I used when I would think about my next husband. I thought "better" as it related to my desire to be married again. I thought "better" when I envisioned myself successfully getting to the other side of this storm. By keeping this scripture in my speech and prayers I began to believe and know that my next EVERYTHING would be better. It literally had me more focused on after the storm to the point where I wasn't focused on the "now" of the storm as much. My next season would be better, my next husband would be better, my next everything would be better. By George, if God didn't perform His word in my life. I am a living testimony of "better is the end of a thing".

Isaiah 40:31 KJV

"But they that wait upon the Lord shall renew their strength; they shall mount up like wings as eagles; they shall run, and not be weary; and they shall walk and not faint."

When I first started dating my first husband, he held the position as minister of music at his father's church. I remember the choir singing this song "They That Wait". I don't know who wrote the music to the song, but the words mirrored this verse. It was sung with a staccato beat and I just loved to sing along. I would stand up and clap my hand and rock back and forth and really enjoy belting out the soprano notes. I'm thankful for that time because, back then, nearly 40 years ago, it was just a song that I loved with a good beat that was sung in church by the choir. What I didn't realize is that God was using my love for the song to deposit His promise in my spirit. I never forgot this song, the scripture, or the promise.

Naturally, when I found myself in this storm, I remember singing this song to God letting Him know that I would wait on Him because this promise in waiting had a return on my investment of the wait. The promise that, when my strength was weak as it was many days; if I waited on Him, then He would renew my strength. But it didn't stop there;

His promise goes on to say that after He renews my weakened strength, He would give wings of an eagle to fly through my trials. Put that check book away, there is more! He promised I would run my race called life and not get weary and ultimately walk and not faint. These were the promises I came to look forward to and this scripture, like all the others, gave me something to hold on to, when I felt like giving up.

Galatians 6:9 KJV

"And let us not be weary in well doing: for in due season we shall reap, if we faint not"

When we go through trials, the tendency to get weary is great. This promise simply says that we will reap if we faint not. This is one of the promises I clung to because the journey to healing God's way became weary for me. I didn't always want to tap into the spiritual; some days I just wanted to be in my flesh and not have God yoke me up. Knowing God and loving Him did not exempt me from this battle between my spirit and my flesh. I had no other choice but to grab a hold of God's word and stand on His promises so that my spirit man showed up every morning and not my flesh. I had to hold on to the fact that my "due season" was coming if I kept going and didn't give up; didn't become weary.

Again, this scripture took me back to my late teenage years when I traveled the country with Rev. Ernest Davis Jr's Wilmington Chester Mass Choir. Keith Pringle had recorded this song called "Let Us Not Be Weary". I loved the beat and whenever we would be in service and a choir sang this song, we would be on our feet singing it. It didn't dawn on me, at that time, that this song was scripture. And, I certainly never imagined that I would ever have to take the words of this song as one of the scriptures that would sustain me during the roughest time of life. I'm thankful for the experience of knowing God's word in song because so many songs I sang growing up I later learned were scriptures. These scriptures became my defense for living in survival mode. So, as I began to search God's word, it became an extreme comfort to me that so many of the songs I sang as a child and in my younger years were scriptures which really helped me hide them deeper in my heart and made them more relatable to me. I'm thankful to God that He gave me what I needed to "not faint". God gave me strength to press forward to my next season and I am now reaping the harvest of blessings because I did not give up.

The message of this entire chapter is "READ THE WORD OF GOD." God speaks through His word and He wants to do such a great work in and through you, but you must read it and spend time with Him to get to know Him for yourself. We are spirit and we are flesh, which ever one you feed the most will be the strongest. When the storms of life come, you want your spirit man strong so that you can endure like a good soldier (2 Timothy 2:3). Our endurance comes from seeking Him. You will find that when you seek Him, He will lead, guide, and direct your life the exact way that He planned from the beginning of time, but you must do your work and read his Word. Doing so will cause you to fall in love with Him and strengthen your walk. When this happens, you will be amazed at who God will send to you to aid them in strengthening their relationship with God. God will literally use your obedience as a tool in His hand to bless other people. It is so rewarding to use your spiritual experiences to bless other people and use your testimony to encourage someone who is going through what you went through. It is God's perfect order for our lives. We are blessed to be a blessing. So, be obedient, study your word so you can obtain strength for the journey through His promises and allow God to use your story for His glory!

STEP FOUR

Walk in Your Healing,

Walk in Victory

"The steps of a good man are ordered by the Lord: and he delighteth in his way." Psalm 37:23 KJV

During this season there was a sister in Christ at my church who we referred to as Jesus' first cousin because everything about her was God-driven and God-focused. I remember it was a running joke of my inner circle, but I really admired her walk. What made her stand out to us was her walk. As much as we laughed and joked about it, the truth of the matter was that she truly exemplified what "walking in victory" looked like. It wasn't that she had never been through anything, it was that she chose Joy despite it!

For me in this season, walking in victory had everything to do with my mental state and how I carried myself. Most of the time I felt like I was walking with a spotlight on my life because of the position I held at my church. At this time, I had just returned from a two-year ministry break. I needed to get away and heal so I was attending another church for healing because I could not continue serving at the capacity in which I was, while going through my divorce because I was hurting so badly. I did not have the emotional fortitude to continue serving in the dance ministry, as lead teacher in youth church for ages 9-12, or to lead praise and worship every Sunday. I loved, loved, loved serving in all these capacities but, when I became broken it was just time to step away and heal.

Following my two-year hiatus from serving, I returned to my church in Delaware and had to find my walk, in healing, and my victory legs. I left married and returned single. That was a significant adjustment for me after being married for 20 years. I remember, one Sunday, my Bishop said, "Singles raise your hands." I was so confused! LOL. I thought to myself, well technically I'm single but I've been married so long I didn't realize I needed to raise my hand. I was really thinking, 'how the heck am I supposed to respond to that God?' Well, after struggling internally in first service, I had gotten my life together by second service and when he asked again (because he was promoting a single's event) I raised my hand, but only slightly-LOL. You see this "walking in victory" thing was easier said than done. I was so proud of myself for getting through the forgiveness phase and had given that so much of my mental space I didn't realize that with forgiveness now behind me I had to walk in my new healing and victory.

It wasn't a comfortable space initially because it was new territory but one thing I knew for sure was I had the victory. Walking it out now meant that I had to cling to God the same way that I had held on to Him at my lowest point. I was now coming out of the devastating pain that gripped my heart for about two years and I knew I was healed but walking in uncharted territory. One thing about serving God and having a relationship with Him was that I knew He had me, and I knew I had to remain connected to the vine so that the vine dresser could guide me in this new walk. I was clay on the Potter's wheel.

My devotions and time with God went from tears and lamenting to worship at a whole new level that I came to love. I was literally living the old cliché that my mother used to say, "Every day with Jesus is sweeter than the day before." My time with God would be so amazing that I would be physically exhausted. I didn't realize then that God was systematically showing me how to walk in my healing and walk in victory. God was saturating my spirit to the brim with more of Him so that, as I walked through this new season, I was able to exhibit so much joy. Talk about unspeakable, unexplainable joy; well I had it but only because I was chasing hard after God's presence in my life. Mainly because chasing after God brought me up from a horrible pit, so I had become addicted to His presence. I, by no means, want to sound self-righteous or holier than thou because I was not. I just knew the formula to successfully walking in my new season of healing and victory and it had everything to do with my time with God.

There is no circumventing time spent with God. PERIOD. It is critical to walking in victory. This is not to say that I didn't have bad days or days when I got into arguments with people who got on my nerves because I did. I had some not so great days in this process of walking in victory and some days I simply got it all wrong. But what I love about God is that His grace and mercy covered and still covers me perpetually. This isn't a license to sin but one to get you free as the gospel group *Commissioned* said in a line from their song, "Back In The Saddle." Not that we take God's grace for granted but God's grace is available to us when we just can't seem to get it right some days and I'm thankful for it personally.

Walking in healing and victory for me now meant learning to become successful in having joint custody of my son versus raising him together with my husband; it meant learning to be successful at being suddenly single and suddenly celibate; it meant being financially responsible for the household all by myself; and now being the spiritual leader of the house. It was daunting, initially, and honestly it wasn't easy finding my victory legs. I had no "on the job" training for this new-found walk, so it was literally baptism by fire with God as my guide.

As it relates to co-parenting my son with a father who now lived in California while I was in Pennsylvania, walking in victory meant being fair and realistic to requests for visits. This was not the time to revert back to bitterness and tell my son's father "no" when he wanted me to allow him to fly my son (alone) across country to California. Talk about walking in healing and victory. I had to send my then 13-year-old, only child, all the way to the other side of the country for him to spend time with his father and new stepmother. So, to be completely transparent, I didn't want to do that. I absolutely did not want him in the house with another woman, nope, DID NOT. I struggled, and I struggled, and I struggled some more. However, because I was spending regular time with God, God really gave me peace and I prayed away all attempts the devil made to throw me back into bitterness and unforgiveness. Why? Because, at the time, my ex-husband had moved on and gotten remarried and I was still single trying to figure it out. Ultimately, I did put my only child on those multiple planes in that season and God was faithful and kept my son safe, THANK YOU JESUS.

As I struggled to do the right thing, God had to yank me by my "spiritual" collar and remind me that my ex-husband was a good person at the end of the day and he loved our son as much as I did, and at age 13 he needed his father more than he needed me. That revelation was such a tough pill to swallow. God had to remind me that there were millions of women across the world who would give anything to have their child's father want to spend time with them, let alone pay hundreds of dollars to fly them across the country to see them several times a year. After wrestling with God on this for a minute, I put my big girl pants on and drove my son to the airport, half the time with a knot in my throat because I knew I would miss him so much, but I did it. I wasn't happy the first few times because I didn't have a life outside of being with him but each time it got easier and easier. Not only did I send him, but I had a conversation with him and demanded that he respect his new stepmother and that he take the time to try and bond with her and develop a relationship with her.

HOWEVER, (if I can have real moment with you) I did tell him that if she did anything out of pocket to him to let me know and I would handle it. Mothers, you already know what I mean because all bets are off when it comes to our children. We do what we have to do and repent later. LOL! Like Eddie Murphy said in one of his movies, "I will cut you and tell the cops you cut yourself shaving and bled to death looking for a tissue." All joking aside, I bless God because there were no issues with his stepmother. She was good a person. God knew what he was doing with that situation is all I will say. This was God showing me again how to walk in healing and victory in this season. If you will allow God to lead you in your victory walk, HE WILL. I am not telling you anything I researched, heard, or read about; I'm telling what I lived. God really saw me through the co-parenting journey and allowed me to walk in healing and victory in this area.

Next thing I did was have a conversation with my spiritual father, Bishop S. Todd Townsend. I told him that my life was an open book to him and I would be open and honest with him about my private life so he and my spiritual mom, Dr. Cleo V. Townsend could keep me accountable and offer guidance and correction where needed and they did. Even though I tried my best to live for God in this season, I could not afford to slip and fall and delay the process of God giving me what I asked for because of disobedience. I intentionally put people in place to keep me accountable. I think every one of my sisters and most of my nieces had keys to my house and they came and went as they pleased so I had to live right cause my family knows how to clown you. LOL!

During this season, if I found myself liking someone (and I did), I would tell my spiritual parents so they could give feedback. AND THEY DID! Truthfully, I had not been single as an adult, so I did not know what I was doing. I started dating my ex-husband at age 16 and we were married at 21 so I had never dated as an adult. I am so thankful God placed them in my life, during this time, to help me navigate my journey to walking in healing and victory. I remember I found myself being enamored with a single, visiting Bishop from another church. I had planned to write him a note but being true to my promise I showed it to my spiritual parents and they lovingly shut that down. Again, thankful that God impressed upon me to surround myself with people who would be honest with me, keep me accountable, and guide me in the right direction. I did not like their answer, but I followed their guidance. This was what walking in healing and victory looked like for me in this season. Learning to wait on God to send my next husband and allowing my spiritual parents to help me not make the wrong move.

Then I started liking another single gentleman at our church. I didn't know this, at the time, but he also was not the one God was sending for me. But at least this time, when I told my spiritual parents, they approved EVENTUALLY. I liked him a lot, but he didn't like me as much as I did him. We were great friends, however, and enjoyed one another's company. We spent time together, though we kept it godly. Truthfully, I was praying and asking God for him to fall in love with me because I was finding myself falling in love with him. However, that prayer DID NOT work because he clearly wasn't falling in love with me. I didn't understand because I thought I was good catch, but I didn't know that God had another plan.

In walks tall, dark, and handsome Darius Nelson. When Darius first asked me out, I was reluctant, but he was persistent. I told him how I felt about this other guy because I was in my late 40's and really not about playing games with people's hearts. Darius' response was, "Well my pursuit of you will either cause him to walk away or step up to the plate." In other words, I ain't going anywhere. What I didn't know was that God had shown me to Darius in a dream. Look here ladies, my Boaz had shown up but because I was being all anxious to be in a relationship, I ALMOST missed him. THAT IS WHY the Bible says, "He that findeth a wife finds a good thing" not "she that falls for someone and tries to make him fall for her." LOL! I must give my husband his props because he pursued me like a real man of God should. He was and still is the perfect gentleman.

I remember telling my spiritual father that Minister Darius asked me out because, as I said earlier, I told him everything as a spiritual daughter who needed accountability. I didn't know what my spiritual father would say because he ALWAYS had jokes. The conversation went like this:

ME: Dad, Minister Darius asked me out to dinner.

HIM: So, what are you going to do?

ME: Go get me a free meal!

We laughed and that was it. I remember going out to dinner with Darius not expecting anything other than getting to know him better as a good friend. God had other plans because the date went very well, and God immediately knit our spirits together. We dated for two years and were married. I truly believe that, as a result of my obedience to God and to follow godly order, I was rewarded with my heart's desire and that is when walking in healing and victory became very real to me.

Then I had to find my financial victory. My ex-husband and I had filed for bankruptcy the year before he left. After he was gone, I had to find resources to pay the mortgage, the bankruptcy court trustee, utilities, food, and all other household expenses. I was overwhelmed financially and ends just were not meeting. My ex-husband had signed the house over to me which made me fully financially responsible. I had to find a way to walk in victory in my finances. I knew enough to pay my tithes and sow sacrificially and I believe that is what got me to the place of making it financially in that season. I was living and breathing Malachi 3:10 (NIV), "Bring the whole tithe into the storehouse, that there may be food in my house. Test me in this," says the LORD Almighty, "and see if I will not throw open the floodgates of heaven and pour out so much blessing that there will not be room enough to store it."

I tested God and not that I got it perfect all the time because there were times that I did not tithe, but God still showed up and showed Himself mighty and strong on my behalf. During this season, the Lord blessed me to be able to raise $2,500 towards a $5,000.00 21-day trip to Europe for my son with People to People International. This was only the grace and favor of God. I desperately wanted my son to have this once in a lifetime experience. He was highly recommended for the program by one of his high school teachers because he was a well-behaved student, so I wanted to make sure he had this experience. God made it happen and I began to see how God was helping me walk in my new-found healing and victory.

Finally, I had to be the new spiritual leader of my house. I had a 13-year-old son in the house and, even though he had been my youth church student for years, I wanted to make sure that he had a private devotional life. I had to seek God for ways to present this to him. It wasn't difficult because he knew the word and he knew how to pray, my God can my son pray! It was now a matter of keeping him accountable and leading our family in consistent devotional time. One of the things I was led to do with him was read through the Bible in a year. So, we purchased a Bible that was specifically designed to help us do exactly that. It was a great experience because whenever we would read a particular text, I would ask him what it meant to him and he would tell me. He was on point most of the time. This led to great discussion about life and how to apply the word. I also would have him read prayers out of John Eckhart's book *Prayers That Rout Demons.* A very effective way to teach children to pray.

Ultimately, I had to learn how to walk into this new season of victory and healing by learning to live my best life without a mate. I learned how to begin to do the things I loved to do. I learned how to hang out with friends and laugh again in my new season and really enjoy myself. I decree and declare that as you walk into a new season of victory and healing and allow God to give you the legs to walk; that you will allow God to show you that life is amazing.

I thank God for all the ways He led me into the new journey of walking in victory and healing. Though challenging at first, and some days extremely difficult, I can't lie; God was faithful to His promise to never leave me nor forsake me. He was right there with me when I got it right, extending grace when I got it wrong (and I did), and probably resting with His hand in His head when I was just way out of pocket some days. All in all, my new walk in victory and healing was a journey that helped me stay healed and whole God's way.

STEP FIVE

Speak Life to Your Situation

"Death and life are in the power of the tongue, and those who love it will eat its fruit."
Proverbs 18:21 NKJV

My first marriage was public and widely known in the gospel community of the Tri-State area (PA-NJ-DE). When it fell apart, I found myself trying to explain what happened to my closest friends and trying to, politely, tell those who did not mean me any good to mind their business. At all times, I tried to be careful about what came out of my mouth. It is so easy to paint ourselves as victims even when we really are victims, but we must be careful not to spit venom on our situation. The enemy uses our emotions to take control of our tongue and causes us to speak doom and gloom over our lives. If you believe what this chapter's scripture says, then despite how badly you are hurting, you will be able to speak life. However, sometimes it is not as easily done as said. This is literally a time in my life when scripture became very real and very applicable. The ability to apply the word of God in difficult seasons is a matter of subduing your flesh long enough to believe that God will perform His word if you trust Him.

Negative words and actions have no place in our situations. We as believers must learn to speak life against all forces of darkness. We must learn to speak life against the desire to have a victim mentality. We must learn to speak life no matter how our actual circumstance appears. Life and death IS in the power of the tongue, so practicing to only speak the promises of God over our lives is critical to our spiritual survival. Remember that we walk by faith and not by sight (2 Corinthians 5:7 KJV). I know it feels like our situation is desolate and undesirable but choosing to speak life over despair will release God to move on your behalf in your situation. We completely tie God's hands from getting involved on our behalf when we speak death to our situation. God is only obligated to move when He is invited to do so, when we quote His promises back to Him. He is not obligated to move nor will He move when we are not actively engaging Him by speaking life.

The ability to speak life requires that we move beyond what we feel in the flesh and tap into the spiritual reality of where we are headed. We are headed towards victory. We are headed towards overcoming this hurt. If we believe what the enemy has whispered in our ears and remain in the flesh, then we begin to speak death. However, if we can find the strength to tap into the spirit and believe that our future is looking better than our current condition and circumstances then we will be able to speak life into our situation. Ecclesiastes 7:8a (NKJV) says, "The end of a thing is better than its beginning." Please know that your victory resides in your future. But only those who speak life and live as though they already have victory are able to reach the victory that resides in their future. Remember, as I just stated, the Bible says that we walk by faith and not by sight. So, to those of us that are spiritual, it really does not matter what our current conditions look like, faith says this too shall pass. Faith says the struggle is over. Faith says I speak life not death into my present condition until my present condition collides with the manifestation of God's promise to heal me. God's ability to heal us is based upon what we speak, and how we respond to our painful situations. God is like a hospital and we are like the wounded on a street corner. Just like a wounded person knows that they must make it to the hospital to have their wounds addressed, we must walk into the hospital of God's word and allow HIM to address our wounds. As it is in the natural, it is so in the spirit. To remain on the street and say, "I'm going to die," is speaking death into your situation. It is only when we pick ourselves up, no matter how difficult, and walk toward our healing that we will ever experience the healing that God has for us.

Isaiah 53:5 (NKJV) says, "But He was wounded for our transgressions, He was bruised for our iniquities; the chastisement of our peace was upon Him; and by His stripes we are healed." This was a daily declaration for me. I would thank God all the time for healing my heart even before it manifested; before the Bahamas trip. I encourage you today to speak life and receive the healing that He has already provided. Know that you are healed, believe that you are healed, speak the words "I am healed." The words you speak have power and when we speak God's word over our lives we are literally tapping into the spiritual realm and manifesting God's will for our lives in the natural realm. It is a powerful thing to be able to tap into. Being able to tap into the unseen to bring manifestation in to the seen is amazing. When you've seen God move by the words you speak once, then you know that He is faithful to move on your behalf every time. Hebrews 4:12a (KVJ) says, "For the word of God is quick, and powerful...." It doesn't always take God a long time to move. In my case, when I made the decision to forgive so I could move forward, God moved quickly on my behalf to heal my broken heart. It all started with me speaking life into my situation. So thankful that I knew just enough of God's word to quote it back to Him which freed Him up to move on my behalf and all because I chose to speak life. My goal is to equip you as well to motivate you to train your tongue and say only what God has to say about your situation. When God is done speaking, then we all need to shut up!

I believe that, when we perceive we are hurt by someone, we fail to realize that the other person is hurting as well. To those of us who were in a marriage, we must realize that just as God loves you and forgives you, God loves and forgives your ex-mate. Let me encourage you to not speak with a bitter tongue against the person that hurt you because, like it or not, they are God's child and He does not take kindly to anyone speaking against His children whether we feel justified in doing so or not. God expects us to speak the truth but speak it in love. Ephesians 4:15 (GW) says, "Instead, as we lovingly speak the truth, we will grow up completely in our relationship to Christ, who is the head." What we speak and how we speak it is so critical to our spiritual development. I know that we experience unbearable pain but understand that we decide how we speak about it. Let me encourage you to speak the truth, but in love. As we learn to do that, the Bible says that we "grow up in our relationship to Christ." If the trials we experience are to grow us up in Christ, then we must put on the proverbial big girl/big boy pants and speak life not death. You can start TODAY. Start to train your mind, spirit, emotions, and tongue to speak life into your situation. It is never too late to begin speaking life, no matter how dire the situation.

I know it isn't easy because, when I was in the heat of anger, I didn't want to speak life because after all, I was angry. I know this book is written from a spiritual perspective and it is real "Jesus-ie" (I know that isn't a word) but the book's subtitle is *Ten Steps to Healing God's Way* for a reason. It's not that I got it right every day because I did not, but on the days I did get it right, it was because I followed the concepts and precepts God laid out for us in His word. So, if you can discipline your mouth to speak life and not death, then you will see God move according to the words you speak. You can't walk around angry and bitter speaking venom in your situation and then go to church and jump and shout at the preached word as if God is going to move for you. The pastor's preached word only works if we work it, not if we scream and shout loud in church. I know I am one of the loudest ones in the sanctuary (trust me I know I am – LOL) but I am loud because I know what speaking life can do. I am a benefactor of speaking life into a situation.

If this is an area with which you struggle, then surround yourself with a village of strong mature believers who can walk along-side you and hold you accountable to the words you speak. If you don't know how to do that, then speak with your pastor at your church about joining the women's ministry, men's ministry, small group ministry or ask about a mentoring program. If you don't have a church home, then I strongly recommend you find a Bible teaching, Bible believing church and join it. Being involved in ministry will expose you to some of God's greatest Christian soldiers who are spiritually mature, and most are more than willing and able to take you under their wing and lead and guide you. Please know that you are stronger with a village to support you. If your current circle of influence does not include a hand full of spiritually mature Christians who can lead you spiritually and keep you accountable to speak life, then it's time to improve your circle. Having a godly village is so critical for spiritual development and for learning to speak life. If you don't have a church home and you don't have an amazing circle of godly wisdom and counsel, then you should really seek God to provide you with a godly village. Everybody needs somebody. Proverbs 11:14b KJV says, "but in the multitude of counsellors there is safety." Get you some friends that love God and will hold you accountable to living for God uncompromised. They will not allow you to speak words that do not edify your situation. They will not be afraid to check you on your speech and correct you when you are talking crazy.

During my season of this trial I was blessed to be surrounded by the best. God showed me how much He loved me by giving me access to my spiritual parents, Bishop S. Todd and Pastor Cleo V. Townsend, the senior pastors of The Resurrection Center in DE. They counseled me, prayed with me, spoke life into me and made sure I watched my words. I also took a break from serving in Delaware and left my church and joined Freedom Christian Bible Fellowship in West Philadelphia under the leadership of Apostle Gilbert Coleman. Apostle Coleman spoke life into me and fed my soul every week. I will never forget his prophesies and his kindness at a time when I was so broken and distraught and needed a godly covering.

I had my spiritual mentor, Prophetess Carmen Austin who stayed in constant communication with me making sure my words were in alignment with where I was headed. She even prophesied to me when I was single about my husband. My God how accurate she was. I had a circle of sisters that included an Elder (Elder Bessie Evans) my Titus 2 covering, a Minister of Music (Kayla Johnson), A Peter (Dana Moore – everybody needs a Peter), My

Smartest Spiritual Sister Friend (Leslie Atley) and a co-Pastor, who was my first prayer partner (Dr. Doris Griffin). My circle was tight then and is even tighter now. My first spiritual parents and these ladies loved God, are full of spiritual wisdom and held me down in the spirit during the most difficult time of my life. They prayed with me, held me up when I felt like I was going to fall and kept me accountable to live for God when I wanted to give up.

I remember being at my first spiritual father's house during this season and saying to him, "And, when my next husband comes..." and I remember him saying to me, "You ready to be married again?" I said yes and I asked God for my next husband every day. I prayed for my man of God. I didn't know who it would be, but I knew he was coming. I knew I had "done my work" to heal my heart and I knew I was free of baggage and drama. God apparently agreed with me because He allowed my spiritual mentor to prophesy to me at her women's retreat that he would come two years before he actually showed up. Elder Carmen was so sure he was coming that she told me to go try on wedding dresses. When the retreat ended and we went back home, Elder Carmen called me on three different occasions and said, "Did you go try on wedding dresses yet?" The first two times I had to say no, but the third time was a charm. So, imagine me going to a few bridal shops, picking out dresses, and trying them on. The bridal shop attendants were asking me the standard questions.

THEM: "So, when did you get engaged?"

Me: "I haven't."

THEM: "Oh, well when is the wedding?"

Me: "I don't know, I don't even have a fiancé!"

THEM: (Complete side eye)

Me: (in my spirit) 'I know what I asked God and I know God hears me.'

A part of me did not care that they thought I was crazy. I think one lady wanted to call the men in white coats for me - LOL. I did not care one bit. When you know what God said and when He confirms it through prophetic word, then you do not really expect the world to understand your actions. Faith is sometimes an action word, so I went trying on wedding dresses like Naaman dipped in the Jordan and the children of Israel marched around Jericho's wall. Both Naaman and the children of Israel, I am sure, felt a little silly at first but in their spirit, they just knew what God said. When you know God and you know what God has said, it does not matter what people say or how they respond to your faith acts. You just know that you know and that is good enough.

It was funny because she prophesied to me at her girlfriend get away in 2009 at Sandy Cove in MD. I will never forget it because it resonated in my spirit so strongly. It was confirmation of me speaking life into my situation consistently for more than two years. I knew I wasn't built to be single so I asked God to teach me whatever lesson I needed to learn in this time of singlehood so I could move on to marriage. I asked God to prepare me for my husband because I wanted to be a great helpmeet. I didn't want to ask God for a husband and not be ready; and, I knew God wouldn't send His best if I wasn't ready so I spoke life and asked God to let me learn my singlehood season lesson quickly so I could move on. God did just what I spoke because "hunty" in 2011 along came this tall, dark, and handsome yumminess that I get to call husband today. We were married two years later and will soon be celebrating our 7th wedding anniversary at the time of writing this.

I want to encourage single ladies who want to be in a relationship, God does not have a shortage of Godly men. God has plenty supply of EVERYTHING, even single godly men. Do not lose heart and don't be discouraged if you want to be married or re-married. Just ask God what you need to do to prepare yourself for the man of God that He wants to send you. I promise you He will not send His best if you are not your best. So, do you want to do the work required for God's best? Just asking (shrugs shoulders)! If so, then just ask God to show you, He will.

The blessing is that, during my time of singlehood, I spoke consistently into the atmosphere what I wanted in a husband. I had the proverbial list! I read lots of books in my season of singlehood because I love books and

I love to read. One of the many books I read was called "Ending the Search for Mr. Right" (How to Be Found by the Man You've Been Looking For) by Michelle McKinney Hammond. In the book, Michelle recommends making a list of things you want in a husband. I made my list and I prayed my list to God. While I wasn't unrealistic in my expectation to find everything on my list, I did have one thing at the number one spot that was non-negotiable: a man that loved and feared God; a man that had his own relationship with God. That is exactly what God sent me in Darius Benjamin Nelson. This is living proof of what God will do for you when you speak life into your situation. I just believed God enough to know that He hears me. Another motivation I had to speak God's word into my situation is found in Psalm 37:4 KJV, "Delight thyself in the Lord and He shall give thee the desires of thine heart." When I first read this text, I said to myself, "WOW God this is a win-win situation." We delight in you, we hope in you, we trust in you; then you will give us the desires of our heart. But as I began to think about this text, I realized that it is still a win-win but delighting and trusting and hoping in the Lord sometimes is easier said than done.

The prince of darkness, the prince of this world has done everything in his power to turn our focus away from delighting in the Lord and hoping and trusting in Him. However, as you learn to adopt a lifestyle of speaking life into your situation, you learn that it becomes a little easier every day to delight ourselves in the Lord. It is really about taking our focus off the things of this world (the natural) and focusing our attention and affection on the things of God (the spiritual) and allowing our speech to line up with the things of God. Literally allowing God to sit on the throne of our heart, learning to adopt a lifestyle of delighting ourselves in Him, and then benefitting from obtaining the desires of our heart. When we delight ourselves in the Lord; The Lord gives us His desires for our hearts and God's desires are what is best for our lives. So, continue to speak life into your situation and allow God to manifest Himself in your words. Your words have power. I will leave you with these verses that encourage you to speak life into your situation:

- 2 Corinthians 4:13 (AMP) "Yet we have the same spirit of faith as he had, who wrote *in Scripture*, 'I BELIEVED, THEREFORE I SPOKE.' We also believe, therefore we also speak,"

- Mark 11:22-24 (NKJV) "So Jesus answered and said to them, "Have faith in God. For assuredly, I say to you, whoever says to this mountain, 'Be removed and be cast into the sea,' and does not doubt in his heart, but believes that those things he says will be done, he will have whatever he says. Therefore I say to you, whatever things you ask when you pray, believe that you receive *them,* and you will have *them.*"

- Proverbs 18:21 (NKJV) "Death and life are in the power of the tongue, and those who love it will eat its fruits."

- Matthew 21:22 (NKJV) "And whatever things you ask in prayer, believing, you will receive."

- Isaiah 55:11 (NIV) "So shall my word be that goes out from my mouth; it shall not return to me empty, but it shall accomplish that which I purpose, and shall succeed in the thing for which I sent it."

Speak life, woman of God!

Speak life, man of God!

Speak life!

STEP SIX

Feed Your Spirit

*"I say then: Walk in the spirit, and you shall
not fulfill the lust of the flesh.
For the flesh lusts against the Spirit, and the
Spirit against the flesh; and these are contrary
to one another, so that you do not do the
things that you wish."*
Galatians 5:16-17 (NKJV)

One of the ways I overcame the extremely strong desire to operate in the flesh was to feed my spirit. As a matter of fact, I had to become obsessed with feeding my spirit because the flesh is a booger! Paul says it best in Romans 7:18-19, (ISV), "For I know that nothing good lives in me, that is, in my flesh. For I have the desire to do what is right, but I cannot carry it out. For I don't do the good I want to do, but instead do the evil that I don't want to do." If we are not careful to continually feed our spirit, before we know it, our flesh rises up and responds to our circumstances and we begin walking down a path that leads to destruction.

Funny thing is the flesh sometimes rises up and responds and without realizing you have done or said something totally crazy or embarrassing. It is at those times that the grace and mercies of God will kick in and save us from ourselves. I am grateful to God for keeping me when my flesh got ahead of my spirit. I always say we are spirit and we are flesh which ever one we feed the most will be strongest and the one that will respond naturally in a crisis. Which are you feeding? Are you feeding your spirit with the things of God that will strengthen and fortify you to fight the spiritual warfare that we all inevitably have to face? Or, are you feeding your flesh with things that will fail you spiritually in a crisis?

There is seemingly a constant war between our spirit and our flesh. Paul broke it down like this in Romans 7:23 (NKJV); *"but I see another law in my members, warring against the law of my mind, and bringing me into captivity to the law of sin which is in my members."* The ability to exercise control of our flesh is a huge advancement toward being able to effectively fight this spiritual warfare of hurt and pain. Unfortunately, we all must navigate through life and sometimes life throws curve balls that we were not expecting, and it feels like we cannot handle it. It feels unfair and it makes you want to give up. I remember having feelings of abandonment, jealousy (as my ex married another woman while I was still single); feelings of suicide; torment, frustration, anger, bitterness, and sheer exhaustion. Some days these feelings would flood my heart at one time, and I would just want to drive my car off a bridge. I mean the pain and hurt of losing all that I lost that year seemed so unfair and I often found myself asking God "Why Me?" I even had my Job moments where I rehearsed to God all the good things I felt I had done for the Kingdom in an effort for God to bring me quick relief.

I like to use this analogy as it relates to spiritual growth. When babies are born, they are either breastfed or bottle fed. The way they grow into adults is to feed them. The better you feed them with good milk and healthy foods the healthier they grow and move onto their next phases in life. Our spirit is the same way. We must feed our spirit in order to grow into healthy spiritual beings. God's expectation is that we stay connected to Him, feeding our spirits daily so that we grow in the grace and knowledge of Him. When we fail to grow spiritually, we literally become spiritually stagnant with our growth. Some of us have not grown spiritually since we accepted Christ because we have been too lazy to do the work. We fuss and we fight; we are easily offended and take to social media all the time with negative posts. That is a clear indication that you need to spend more time with God and grow up a little more, spiritually. No shade at all but I just want to stress the importance of us all building a perpetual system of spiritual growth and development in our lives. In 1 Corinthians 3:2, Paul expresses his desire to give solid food to his followers but could not and had to feed them milk because they were spiritually unprepared for solid foods. My prayer and desire for you in your season of difficulty, and every season of your life is that you will be intentional about feeding your spirit so that you are growing up in Christ daily and becoming stronger and stronger in the things of God.

The danger of not feeding your spirit with the things of God is that, when the storms of life are raging, your flesh rises up and typically causes you to do things that are outside of the will of God. The WORST place to be in a storm is outside of the will of God. I know the feeling of hurt and pain, and I know what it is to feel like you did not deserve it. However; if you can just muster up the strength to feed your spirit with the things of God and demand of your schedule to spend daily time in His presence, then I promise you God will give you the strength that you need to fight God's way. Unbelievers fight in the natural and spin their wheels for years and it gets them nowhere. However, we, as believers, fight the good fight of faith in the spirit realm, but we can only successfully accomplish this if our spirit is strong!

So, what does feeding your spirit look like and how do you get into God's presence when you can barely breathe? I will walk you through what I did to, hopefully, provide guidance. In seasons of life when everything was turned upside down, having resources to help get your spirit in alignment with God is so very critical. Below are some of the things I did that helped strengthen me, spiritually:

➢ **Fasting** – Matthew 17:21 (NKJV) says "This kind does not go out except by prayer and fasting." Sometimes you have to take a break from things that tend to impede your ability to hear from God. While food doesn't stop you from hearing God, I believe that sacrificing a significant physical need like eating sends a message to God that we are serious about our request. I believe fasting gets God's attention because just as Jesus sacrificed his life for us and it caused God to move in a mighty way; the same goes for turning a plate down and praying to the God who is able to do exceedingly and abundantly above all that we can ask or think. Fasting is the pattern that God set in His word for us to be able to have Him move on our behalf. Fasting and prayer together is one of the best ways to feed your spirit. It does major damage to the kingdom of darkness and it opens your spiritual ears so that you can clearly hear from God. The Bible is clear, ALL THINGS COME THROUGH FASTING AND PRAYER! My times of fasting and prayer opened up another avenue for communion with God that took me to another level in my relationship with Him.

➢ **Devotion** – devotion is defined as "religious worship or observance." Taking time for private worship and reading of God's word is an amazing way to feed your spirit. It is literally spiritual food that strengthens your spirit man. It shifts your atmosphere and changes your focus and improves your mood. Overall, regular and consistent devotions keep you grounded and focused on your relationship with God and allows you to go deeper and deeper into the mysteries of God. During this time, I used CeCe Winans "Throne Room" as my 'go to' devotional worship music. It just put me in a place that allowed me to enter God's presence and simply worship. Most days I didn't enter with a long list of complaints or what I was going through, but it was simply a time for me to forget about myself and concentrate on the goodness of God. There is something about quality alone time with God that really lifts and encourages the soul. It is difficult to put into words, but it is cleansing and impactful and empowering. Good quality time in the presence of God where you are simply there because you want to enjoy HIS good company will leave you feeling as if you can run through troops and leap over walls. Finding time for daily devotion can be challenging but just like you find time to feed your natural man, it is equally as important that we find time to feed our spirit man by spending time with God daily, especially when we are in the midst of a storm. Laying on my face, listening to worship music and whispering sweet words of worship to God became my norm. I remember one night it got so good that hours had passed by and I didn't even know it. When I came out of God's presence it was morning and time to wake my son up for school. That's the kind of time with God we need to get through life's very difficult hurts, but we must make the decision to make it a priority. Watching your favorite shows on TV or scrolling through the internet sometimes MUST take a back seat to feeding and strengthening our spirit. It's a decision that we choose to make. Whether it is getting up an hour early or staying up an hour late, whatever sacrifice is needed to make it work for your life is very much worth it. The greatest thing about devotions is, the more time you spend with God, the more time you want to spend with God. You literally have a "wow I should have had a V8 moment" (I'm dating myself – but if you know what I am talking about you're old too! LOL). In other words, you literally want to smack yourself on the head for procrastinating on spending devotional time with God because it's just really, really, good. Wayne Huirua put it beautifully in his book *Rebranding Worship*

- o **"A worshipper sees what God sees; they see other people and situations through God's eyes, but also when looking into a mirror.......A worshipper gives**

up his own view and adopts that of his heavenly Father, including his or her view of themselves."

This hit me like a ton of bricks because it really explains my ultimate goal in life. I want to feed my spirit to the point where I see everything through God's eyes. I want to see me how God sees me when I look in the mirror. I want to see other people through God's eyes so that I share His love and His compassion with them. This is a real goal that I am striving for every day. Not that I get it right every day because I don't, but this is a declaration that I keep before me and feed it to my spirit on a regular basis.

➤ **Listening to The Word** – I have been in church since I was an embryo! Some of you will catch that later. LOL! I remember as a little girl sitting in church (there was no youth church back then, so you went to Sunday School before worship but you sat your tail in worship and you had better be quiet!) really enjoying my pastor, the late Bishop Robert F. Walters (Presiding Prelate of the African Union Methodist Protestant Church), as he preached. He was charismatic in his delivery, and I remember how his sermons were filled with the word of God, they were meaty. I can still quote Psalm 103:8-13 today because I distinctly remember him quoting that passage of scripture frequently from the pulpit. I can hear it like it was yesterday. Then, as I grew in my walk with God and began traveling the country with The Rev. Ernest Davis Jr.'s Wilmington Chester Mass Choir, I remember being exposed to some of the best preaching I ever heard. I fell in love with the preached word of God, I fell in love with the skillful delivery of it. I love hearing the preached word of God. During this season of my life, I was on sabbatical from my set place where my Bishop S. Todd Townsend, Sr. was a preaching machine. I needed a place to heal from all I was enduring, and I landed at Freedom Christian Bible Fellowship in Philadelphia, PA where, at the time, Bishop Gilbert Coleman was the pastor. Apostle now but Bishop then, spoke into my life through the word of God in such a powerful way. God used him to prophesy to me on several occasions and the accuracy was amazing. I would purchase CDs and listen to Apostle preach repeatedly. Listening to the preached word of God is a great way to feed your spirit. I have so many scriptures in my spirit not just from reading the word but from listening to the preached word. A good preached word of God has healing, delivering, and saving power. It does not replace studying your word, but it does provide insight, confirmation and revelation at a level not achieved by reading the word alone. My absolute all-time favorite preacher during this season was Bishop T. D. Jakes. I was an Aaron's Army partner at the time, and I received preaching CD's in the mail monthly for my monthly donations. The sermons he preached in this season literally kept me from taking my life. I was feeding my spirit by listening to the Word of God, consistently and in multiple ways. Some nights I would put a sermon on and watch it over and over. Other nights I would put the word of God on and let it play while I slept. I played preaching CD's in the car, preaching CD's at work, preaching

CD's while I cooked, etc. I was deliberate about what was going into my ear and eye gates because the devil was crouching at the door waiting for a way into my spirit so he could destroy me. He knew what God's assignment on my life was and he did everything he could in this season to kill me. BUT GOD! SIDEBAR: the only downside of listening to that much word is when you are filled with the Holy Ghost, it can become a problem at work when the spirit hits you! (LOL you gotta be careful in these spirit-filled streets! LOL!) Be that as it may, I strongly believe it was my deliberate and calculated persistence to FEED MY SPIRIT with the word of God, whether preached or read, that got me through this season. And, it was my amazing devotional life that shortened my storm.

> **Journaling** – Journaling is defined as a record of experiences, ideas, and reflections kept for regular or private use; an account of day to day experiences. During this time of my life, while going through this storm, I was a member of The Resurrection Center in

Wilmington, DE. My amazing leaders, Bishop S. Todd Townsend and his equally amazing wife, Dr. Cleo V. Townsend always encouraged all their leaders to journal. Journaling was not a foreign concept to me because I journaled as a teenager but as an adult it initially felt juvenile. However, I quickly adopted the practice of doing it especially when I would read my word. The closer you get to God in your walk with Him, the more He speaks to you and it just seemed that when I began journaling as a leader in the church, God would speak. I would open the Bible to the same passages I had previously read, and He would say something different every time. Journaling was my way of documenting what God was speaking to me in that season. It was amazing and I was fully enjoying it. However, God really challenged my love for journaling during this storm because I did not want to write. I was used to journaling when all was right with the world and my journal entries were always positive, uplifting and filled with worship. It was a "tip toe through the tulips" season of my life. HOWEVER, when my "life got flipped, turned upside down," I did not feel there was anything to journal about. I was not at all interested in rehearsing my pain through journaling. Nope, wanted nothing to do with it. Well, God led me to a prayer journal called "A Personal God" by Keri Noble during one of my almost daily visits to Barnes and Noble. God knew exactly what I needed! This prayer journal was indescribably amazing. It was an extremely organized journal with dividers on topics of prayer. It gave wisdom and insight on prayer and gently led you to journal your prayer life. I was completely blown away at how I would start journaling a prayer to God that started with me complaining about what I was going through but before I knew it each journaled prayer ended in words of gratitude, thankfulness, and worship. This journal was just what I needed to keep me focused during this time of emotional uncertainty. Something I found to be true through my prayer journaling experience is that, when God is your foundation and you hit rock bottom (which I had), you hit God. I do not know about anyone else, but I would rather run into God during a storm than anything else. The combination of God as my foundation and the way this journal guided me completely shifted the focus away from complaining. From there it really opened me up to a love of purging my thoughts and making my requests known. I read an article about Journaling called "What's All This About Journaling" written for the New York Times website by Hayley Phelan on October 25, 2018. This article explains that journaling is a panacea (a solution or remedy for all difficulties or diseases) for modern life. It has been known to boosts mindfulness, memory, and communication skills. It goes on further to explain that it helps us get better sleep, which promotes a stronger immune system and boosts self-confidence, as well as improve our IQ. New Zealand Researchers suggest it may even help heal wounds faster. Whatever the benefits various researchers and journalist have found, for me personally it was soul cleansing self-care and a way to purify my heart toward God. It allowed me to empty my spirit and thoughts of all the junk and baggage that comes with being hurt, angry and bitter. I strongly suggest journaling as a way of feeding your flesh. If you have not done so, I highly recommend giving it a try. You might like it and so will your spirit man. One great thing about journaling is that for the most part, you are writing for your eyes only, so it really takes the pressure off trying to be the perfect writer. Unless you are journaling as part of an assignment for a course, journaling is just between you and God. It is private, so improper English and bad grammar have no role in journaling. Enjoy the journey if you have not done so already. If you do not know where to start, then simply purchase a blank journal book. Select one that you really like. I prefer wire bound and I like a nice scripture on the outside and a scripture on every page. Some of you may need to start with a prayer or other subject-focused journal that guides you through a spiritual focus and thought daily. Sometimes, that is needed when you have a lot going on and can't really get your thoughts out on paper. Whatever type you decide to use, just start and let God guide you through it.

➢ **YouVersion** – If you have not done so already, download the YouVersion app. YouVersion is a free bible app that has several versions of the Bible, but it also includes reading plans on a wide variety of subjects. I've completed reading plans on YouVersion that include everything from Marriage Ministry to Worship. The topics are limitless and, more recently, more popular personalities in the Christian Culture have authored a few reading plans. Gospel Artist such as David and Tamela Mann as well as Charles Jenkins have written reading plans. Most plans come with daily reading that won't take any more than 10-15 minutes to read. Plans come with a devotion/focus and accompanying scriptures. Another great feature is it allows you to do a reading plan with a bunch of friends. This is a great way to have your village that I discussed prior, keep you accountable to growing and feeding your spirit. I love YouVersion and you will as well so if you don't have it on your mobile device please download it today. It is easily accessible via your handheld device so you can access it any time of day. THANK ME LATER! YOU'RE WELCOME!

This step of feeding your spirit will really help you in your healing process and you will soon see the spiritual growth and development that is inevitable, if you are diligent and persistent in this process. I was literally blown away at the level of growth I achieved simply by longing and thirsting for God. God has a way of quenching your thirst for Him in ways that will cause you to fall in love with Him all over again. However, I won't assume that everyone reading this book already has a relationship with God and we will get to that later but let my life be an example to you of the benefits of having a great relationship with God.

God truly kept me alive and well during a time in my life when I thought all hope was lost. A time when I no longer wanted to live. I wanted to take the easy way out because I did not want to be stretched nor challenged. I didn't want to go through it. But we must realize that, in order for a flower to release its wonderful aroma, it must be crushed; in order to get olive oil, the olive must be hard pressed. It is during the most difficult times of our lives that we learn how to fight in the spirit; it is in these times that we learn just how amazing

God is and how it is He who is fighting for you and keeping you in the battle. You will win and you will overcome this hurt and pain of life that you are experiencing. Just keep living because this too shall pass. It will get greater later.

King Solomon said it like this in Ecclesiastes 7:8a KJV "better is the end of a thing than the beginning thereof." God is basically promising us that it will be better in the end. I took a hold of this verse some days during my trial and hung onto it for dear life. It actually was the beginning of my life of daily declarations. I remember saying to God, in prayer one day, *"God you said better is the end of a thing"* and then it dawned on me that it was a declaration. Because life and death is in the power of the tongue, I realized that saying "better is the end of a thing" was an actual declaration of my expectation that things would get better. I began to believe it and began declaring "and, when my next husband comes…." Man, oh man let me tell you how God is true to His word and daily declarations work. I'm now married to a tall, dark and handsome man of God who loves God as much as I love Him and effectively washes me with the water of the word. I am thankful that I fed my spirit during this season because it kept me alive long enough for my Boaz to find me. I said all that to say, you will not die but live. Feed your spirit and keep living, my friend.

STEP SEVEN

Don't Allow the Enemy In

And Jesus answered and said to Him, "Get behind Me, Satan! For it is written, 'You shall worship the Lord your God, and Him only you shall serve.'" Luke 4:8 (NKJV)

The enemy is crafty and deceitful above all. He knows exactly how to tempt you and with what to tempt you. If the enemy came at Jesus like he did in the wilderness, then please know that He is coming after you even stronger. I submit to you today that you do not allow the enemy to control any part of your situation or circumstance. Even though it may feel good for a short time to get revenge on the person that hurt you, please know that vengeance belongs to the Lord. When we take matters into our own hands, we take it out of God's hands. Trust me when I tell you that you need God's hands all over your situation because, left to our own devices, we will mess it up every time.

In my case, the enemy did try to enter my situation through revenge a little but more strongly by speaking suicide to me. I can vividly recall how the enemy gave me specific instructions on how to kill myself. One evening, I remember being so distraught by all that I was going through that I actually went into my kitchen, found the sharpest knife, went upstairs into my bedroom, and laid the knife on the nightstand. I stared at it for most of the evening crying and trying to write suicide letters to all my closest family members and friends. BUT GOD is good because there were just too many letters that needed to be written and I got exhausted even thinking about how large of a village I had. However, I thank God for Jesus who is my Savior because, as I contemplated escaping the pain, God reminded me ever so gently of Job and how before the enemy could lay a finger on Job he had to go to God and get permission. God also reminded me that there was NO ONE on the face of this earth that could raise my son as well as I could. I was strengthened by that because I knew that what I was going through, no matter how difficult, was for the glory of God. At that point, I was determined to not let God down and to make Him a proud Father. The enemy came close that day to entering my situation and ending my life, but I thank God for Jesus who gave me strength to shut him all the way down.

I just want to encourage you today in case the enemy is speaking to you the way he spoke to me. Nothing can happen to you that God does not allow. I know what we go through doesn't make sense to us and we feel like our situation is the worst thing in the world but, as long as God is on the throne, and (Thank You Jesus) HE still is, you are never alone. The enemy is a wicked, foul, tormenting spirit and he tries to destroy the people of God who are destined to birth their purpose, but thanks be to God who always causes us to TRIUMPH! God promised that He would never leave us nor would He ever forsake us. I promise you, if you hold on, God will deliver.

If you cry out to Him from the depths of your soul, HE will respond. A songwriter wrote, "It is no secret what God can do. What He's done for other's He'll do for you." God is no respecter of persons; if He delivered me, I promise and guarantee you He will deliver you so please do not allow the enemy in to kill you but instead rise up and know that the enemy is a defeated foe. The enemy's only power is deception. He deceives well but he has no power over you whatsoever. Please believe that. He is a toothless lion and a powerless wizard.

We must remain prayed up and begin practicing the art of praying without ceasing. The stronger the enemy tries to encroach upon our situation, the more we must pray and seek God for strength to fight and spiritual discernment to recognize the enemy's tricks. Spiritual discernment is key to knowing when the enemy is trying to sneak in so that you know how to respond. Please believe that, because God is bigger, better, and stronger than the enemy, you will survive. I know it is easier said than done and I know we grow weary when it seems like we have been going through it for a long time, but we must never give up on God because He has never given up on us. There is purpose in your pain, purpose in your press and purpose in your persistence. Someone is in desperate need for you to make it out of this painful situation because they will need you to minister to them at a level that no one else can. If you are experiencing a painful situation right now, it is more than likely that God has you on a healing assignment. This is necessary because only you will be able to identify with and minister to the pain of those assignments He is sending your way in the future.

Only you will be able to walk alongside your assignment as they fight. Your ability to keep the enemy out of your fight means you are literally equipping yourself to help someone else do the same. It blows my mind how God sends women for me to minister to or pray over whose situation is almost identical to mine. When I share my story with them, some of them just start crying and they are mostly encouraged by the fact that I made it out and succeeded (most days) at keeping the enemy at bay. When you understand how to fight your battles, then you win.

Michael W. Smith, my favorite Christian Contemporary Music (CCM) song writer penned a song called "Surrounded." The hook of the song says, "it may look like I'm surrounded but I'm surrounded by YOU." No matter what the enemy tries to do to your spirit man, you must adopt the attitude that God has you surrounded. The devil would have you believe that he has you surrounded but look again, there is a host of angels surrounding the enemy ready to fight on your behalf. In 2 Kings 6, the prophet Elisha was being attacked by the King of Syria because the prophet Elisha kept warning the King of Israel of the king's plan to attack Israel. The King of Syria was so frustrated with Elisha that he sent a strong army force after Elisha. When Elisha's servant, Elijah, saw the army of horses and chariots surrounding the city he became afraid but the prophet Elisha told him, "Do not be afraid, those who are with us are more than those who are with them." So it is for us, the angels that God sends to surround us is greater than the enemy and God is using our angels to keep our enemy at bay so DO NOT let the enemy in by what you say out of your mouth (because your words have power) or your actions. Sometimes, we react to things in the flesh and it sets our healing process on a trajectory that veers off course from where God wants us.

Do not let the enemy in by how you respond to his attempts of attack (greater is He that is in us than He that is in the world). Know who you are and know what you have access to. You are the righteousness of God and you have access to His strength and His spirit to get you through any situation or attack from the enemy. Use it to win this fight. It may look like a fight in the natural but it is spiritual warfare and you win when you are able to know that those who are with you (angels) are more than those who are with them (the enemy of our soul). You must keep the devil out. Remember we don't wrestle with flesh nor blood but against powers and principalities and spiritual wickedness in high places. But do not give in, keep fighting in the spirit because that is how we keep the enemy out of our situation and circumstance. Don't lose sight of the goal. The goal is for you to get healed from this hurt so you can help others. Remember when you are strengthened, strengthen your brother (Luke 22:32). The enemy will attempt to distract you, but your fight is fierce, and you will win. So, when the enemy sends a co-worker to betray you or lie on you, just remember that our weapons are not carnal (natural) but mighty through God to the pulling down of strongholds. It's spiritual, it's spiritual, it's spiritual. You will not win in the flesh. Cussing that co-worker out means the enemy won and you've lost your witness for God. However, holding your peace and allowing God to fight your battles means you will win, and God will show up on your behalf every time. Try it and see. It works.

The devil is very good at sneak attacks. One day during this season he almost got me, I had a misunderstanding with an individual and this person was angry at me. I mean this person was like a horse at the gate ready to come out and trample me. Just like a horse breathing heavy in anticipation of the race, this person was hurling threats and inaccurate accusations. My initial thought was to lash out, respond, and say something hurtful and threaten them as they had threatened me. I was so angry and so ready for the fight in the flesh. Seriously, I wanted to punch this person in the throat just so they would shut up. I saw myself choking them until they turned red, not purple, just red then I would let go. LOL! On top of that, the enemy was giving me the best come backs with words that would have cut that person to the core. HOWEVER, there comes a time in your walk with God when you know and understand that it is the enemy luring you into a trap. 2 Corinthians 2:11 (CSB) says, "so that we may not be taken advantage of by satan, for we are not ignorant of his schemes." The enemy is always looking to take advantage, always looking to trip us up and cause us to fall. That day, I am glad to report, I passed the test. I took the high road, begrudgingly subdued my flesh (which was on fire) and shut my mouth even though I was about to explode. I found a quiet place and went to talk to God about it. Was this easy? Heck NO! I just was depending on God to do so much for me at this time that I was not trying to upset or disappoint God. Ultimately, I came to the realization that the person was dealing with deep rooted anger and bitterness from years ago that was left unresolved. We all know that hurt people hurt people and this person was a ticking bomb, so I just bowed out gracefully. Prayed that God would heal the persons deep rooted hurts and moved on. Besides, I read this quote by Mark Twain:

> Never argue with a fool, onlookers may not be able to tell the difference.
> — Mark Twain

God forbid if an onlooker would think I was a fool. Not giving anyone that level of satisfaction. I am grateful that I passed the test that day because there were plenty of other days that I failed the test, fell off the wagon, and rolled down the hill. SMH!

Isaiah said, when the enemy comes in like a flood the spirit of the Lord would raise up a standard against him. (Isaiah 59:19b) BUT, when the enemy is trickling in versus coming in like a flood, I believe God fully expects you to be able to handle that after we get to a certain place in our walk with Him. Let's stop failing at what I like to call the trickle test. God wants us to win the small battles on our own. You know, the ones that He is sure are minor enough for you to handle. God already knew what we were up against and has already prepared the way for when the enemy tries to enter our situation. Tap into the spiritual realm and allow God to give you the fight plan. God's way is the only way we win, and we win when we can effectively keep the devil out!

STEP 8

Know That God Has A Plan

"For I know the thoughts that I think toward you, says the Lord, thoughts of peace and not of evil, to give you a future and a hope."
Jeremiah 29:11 (NKJV)

Before the foundation of the worlds were framed, God knew you. He knew when you would be born, who your parents would be, where you would live and everything you would go through. Nothing takes God by surprise. God was very strategic in planning your life and supplying what you would need to make it through the hard times. He sets people in our paths to give us the word of encouragement we need just when we need it because our lives have a plan. He provides unmerited favor when we face impossible situations and He lavishes us with loving kindness, when we deserve judgement, because He has a plan. God is simply amazing and His love for us is amazingly overwhelming because He has a plan.

I recently saw this diagram. It depicts what our plan looks like versus what God's plan looks like. Our plan = a straight line between points A and B. Simple right? LOL

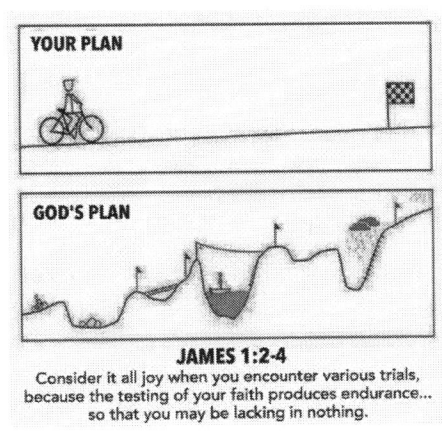

JAMES 1:2-4
Consider it all joy when you encounter various trials, because the testing of your faith produces endurance... so that you may be lacking in nothing.

However, God's plan is this crazy line with high peaks and deep valleys that looks like the line on the heart monitor of someone having mild heart attacks. LOL. This diagram is so accurate and on point. We always see our plan as a straight line between two points. As a matter a fact, we are taught in algebra that the shortest distance between two points is a straight line so why would we not think that we can reach our destination by going in a straight line? Herein lies the problem, folks. We always want to take the easiest, shortest route; a shortcut. I remember reading a book with my praise team years ago called "What to Wear to War" by Warren Wiersbe. One of my favorite chapters in the book was titled "Shortcuts Take Too Long." God has a plan for our lives, but we must take His route. His route is sometimes not easy, does not make sense, feels unfair, and is difficult when we try to do it without Him. The enemy would have us believe that we save time when we take short cuts, but evidence shows that this thought process sinks ships. Think about the pharmaceutical company that took short cuts to develop a drug which hit the market and ultimately ended up killing people. Think about the finance company that took a short cut, reporting their earnings dishonestly in an effort to increase their market value so investors would invest in them only to find out they lied and are unable to pay dividends and their company crumbles. Car manufacturers who take short cuts in engineering a vehicle have repeatedly put cars on the market that failed, and in some cases took people's lives. All of these are examples of how taking a short cut will prolong your process. In each instance listed above someone was injured, lost their life, lost their life savings, or experienced some other irreversible loss.

Many times, this is simply because people are generally impatient and don't want to wait for the time it takes to make something great. We have adopted this microwave mentality towards running this life and that just isn't the way God designed it. It takes time for God to develop you into who you are called to be. Don't settle for a happy meal when God has a whole Thanksgiving Dinner complete with five cheese macaroni (LOL, Victory In Christ Christian Center insider). Wait on God's plan to be revealed to you so you can run with patience this race that is set before you. (Hebrews 12:1b) A half-baked cake is just nasty. Wait on the Lord and His plan for your life and be of good courage. You are great in God's eyes because God created you and He does not make junk. He has a plan for you, but will you submit your will to Him? Will you seek Him with your whole heart through worship? Will you sustain daily devotion and reading His word to get a download of His plan for your life? Will you wait on Him to reveal His plan? Or, will you try to carve out your own godless life plan without Him? God knows you better than you know yourself ("you don't even know who you are!" in my Lion King Rafiki voice). You are amazing, you are awesome, and you are incredible but continue to marinate in God's training process for your life until God is ready to reveal who you are to the world. Don't get ahead of God's plan for your life because when you go before Him you go without Him. And, do not go without Him because the safest place in the whole wide world is in the will of God. Stay with God, stay in His will, stay with His plan and not your own. You may be saying, "Well what is God's plan for me?" Glad you asked, the answer to that question lies within your devotion and worship time. During this time, there should be a two-way conversation with God. We talk to God then we shut up and let Him respond. God will speak to you if you will listen. He will answer if you quiet your spirit and tap into the well of His presence. Again, we have developed a microwave mentality toward spending time with God. No need to fear God's presence, He already knows the things you try to hide from Him. Besides, God's perfect love casts out all fear (1 John 4:18). Don't be "skurd"!! LOL. God loves you and wants only the very best for you, but you must crucify your flesh and let God drive. God's plan is for you to prosper and be in good health (3 John 1:2).

I believe our biggest challenge in trusting God's plan for our lives is having bought into the world's system of how things are supposed to be done. We trust the demonic systems in place that the enemy has set as a trap for us instead of seeking God for His plan for our lives. Remember God's ways (plans) are not our ways and His thoughts are not our thoughts. His ways (plans) are greater, His thoughts are greater than ours will ever be. Your heartache or trial is never wasted. God will use it for His glory. I found this to be true because of how God used my pain to help other people. I had no idea what His plans were, but they were ultimately working for my good. When I was going through my storm, there were times I thought I would not make it. I thought I would die. Now I know why God chose to carry me some days but back then I felt like I had been thrown in the lion's den not knowing God had a plan. Please believe that God's plan will only prosper you and not harm you; God's plans will give you a bright future and great hope! They go beyond your wildest dreams.

Chapter 9

Be Strong

"Have I not commanded you? Be strong and of good courage; do not be afraid, nor be dismayed, for the Lord your God is with you wherever you go." Joshua 1:9 (NKJV)

In this text, God is speaking to Joshua and providing instruction and encouragement as he takes over leadership of the Israelites after Moses death. The task ahead of Joshua was daunting indeed. Because God knew the number of enemies that would rise up against Joshua, He wanted to encourage Joshua from the beginning to "be strong and know the I am with you wherever you go." Please know that, in whatever trial you may be facing, God is with you always. He is fighting WITH you. And, those times when you feel you can't fight and need a quick break, God will fight FOR you. I love the Israel Houghton song "In Jesus Name." The chorus says, *"God is fighting for us pushing back the darkness lighting up the kingdom that cannot be shaken. In the name of Jesus, enemy's defeated, and we will shout it out, shout it out."* God is on our side and He is fighting for us and with us, but we can't walk around with the mentality that God is going to do EVERYTHING for us. Even though He is capable, some battles God fully expects us to be strong enough to fight on our own. Will we be afraid? Yes! Will we want to turn back? Absolutely! However, we must fight anyway. As we journey through life and become spiritually stronger because we are spending regular quality time with God, we get to a point in our spiritual growth and development that we can handle certain things because God has equipped us to do so.

For example, in the natural, I am confident that my son can cook, clean and groom himself. If, at 27 years old, he called me asking me to come and cook for him, clean for him, or pick out his clothes for him, then most people would find that to be strange.

Rightly so, because he spent his formative years with me and I taught him how to do those things by demonstrating them to him and monitoring him to make sure he could do it because our job as parents is to train our children in such a way that they can survive if we are not around. It is so in the natural and it is so in the spirit realm. God feels like we should fully be able to handle some skirmishes with the enemy. The problem is some of us have stopped developing spiritually as Christians so, when we are confronted with a small skirmish, we are unable to handle it. As a result, we fall prey to the enemy's attack by resorting to the flesh to fight instead of tapping into our spiritually mature selves and kicking the devil in the gut. All the strong soldiers wave your hands in the air and HOLLA!! Just in case you are thinking, 'Well where is that in scripture?' Glad you asked. Hebrews 5:12 (NIV) says, "In fact, though by this time you ought to be teachers, you need someone to teach you in the elementary truths of God's word all over again. You need milk, not solid foods." My God today, as the seasoned saints would say. Let us not digress in our spiritual growth, or even become stagnant, but let us chase after God and our spiritual growth and development in a way that produces a life of perpetual growth in God.

Again, there are certain lessons we should have learned and should be teaching others, but the reverse often happens, and you AGAIN need to be taught the basics of God's word. No shade, we have all had phases of our walk with God in which growth wasn't always happening, that has been my testimony as well from time to time. But, God says, you should be able to eat meat, but you are still on milk. Visually, imagine a 6-year old walking around with a bottle of milk not able to eat meat? We would automatically think something is wrong developmentally with that child. That is how some Christians are right now. We have been saved for 40 years and we are still mad at the usher that would not let us sit on the front row 30 years ago. God is really looking for us to grow into His grace and knowledge so that we are strong enough to fight the enemy. He is looking for us to be spiritually stronger this year than we were last year. Sometimes, we wonder why our test and trials last so long. It may just be that we haven't learned what God is trying to teach us, so we have to keep repeating the test. What God has for us is so amazing, He simply will not allow us to have it until we are spiritually mature enough to handle it, strong enough to keep it and not break it. I remember listening to a sermon during this time in my life (don't ask me who said it because I was listening to about 10 different preachers then) but he/she basically said, "You elongate the storm because you ain't learning what God is trying to show you." I remember immediately adding this sentence to my prayer time, "God, whatever I am doing to prolong this storm, please show me what I need to do in order for you to say "peace be still." We all know that, into each life, rain must fall but how long it rains depends on us most of the time. God, help us to learn the lesson and agree with and obey You quickly. If we learn the lessons God plans for us and pass the tests quickly, it will strengthen us and equip us to fight. While the enemy has built his dark kingdom on this earth, be of good cheer because heaven is God's throne and the earth is His foot stool, so the enemy's kingdom is under God's feet! SHONDO!!! (insert hands up emoji!). I was fortunate enough to travel the country with gospel music's premier (in my humble opinion), Stellar Award-winning, Rev. Ernest Davis Jr's Wilmington Chester Mass Choir. One of the songs we were blessed to record was called "Strong" written by Ricky Grundy and the chorus says,

My spirit won't be discouraged. His grace and power will deliver. No weapon formed against me shall have victory over this life. Just to think unconditional love wins the fight. For when I am weak then I'm made strong!

"For when I am weak, then I'm made strong (2 Corinthians 12:9a)." God will make you strong where you are weak and uphold you with His mighty right hand. God has placed everything inside of us that we need to make it. When I look back on my trial, I am simply amazed at the strength God gave me to endure. I am amazed that God kept me strong and I am standing here today because I had just enough sense to grab ahold of Him and He made me strong. God is a constant reminder of His ability to keep us when we need Him most. God is so interested in making us strong and fit for battle. He is heavily invested in us and left us the pattern for strength and endurance with His example of how He endured the cross and crucifixion. He took every lash of the cat of nine tails because of His Love for us but it was such a great demonstration of how strong we can be because of Him.

My mother used to tell me that God doesn't need coward soldiers. My former Bishop, Dr. S. Todd Townsend, Sr., always told us, "go scared." I understand that statement in an entirely different way today. I believe that statement infers that God needs some soldiers that can get through the battle without giving up and without allowing the enemy to kill them. The enemy has clearly waged war on the saints but what our heavenly Father is looking for are a few good soldiers. He needs the type of soldiers that are strong enough to fight through the worst of the war and still come out victorious. He is looking for the type of soldier that Gideon took into battle (Judges 6-8; this story is told in three chapters – yup, read it, it's a good read). The type of soldier Gideon took into battle, they are ones that stayed ready. They never took their hands off their weapons not even to drink water from the brook. God is looking for strong soldiers who stay fight ready, they don't take their hands off their weapons and can kick the devil in his teeth at a moment's notice. How do we stay war ready? The answer is found in Ephesians 6:10-18 NKJV

The Whole Armor of God

Finally, my brethren, be strong in the Lord and in the power of His might. Put on the whole armor of God, that you may be able to stand against the wiles of the devil. For we do not wrestle against flesh and blood, but against principalities, against powers, against the rulers of the darkness of this age, against spiritual hosts of wickedness in the heavenly places. Therefore, take up the whole armor of God, that you may be able to withstand in the evil day, and having done all, to stand. Stand therefore, having girded your waist with truth, having put on the breastplate of righteousness, and having shod your feet with the preparation of the gospel of peace; above all, taking the shield of faith with which you will be able to quench all the fiery darts of the wicked one. And take the helmet of salvation, and the sword of the Spirit, which is the word of God; praying always with all prayer and supplication in the Spirit, being watchful to this end with all perseverance and supplication for all the saints.

This text was a compass for me on not only how I should stay strong but also what to wear to this ongoing war. Knowing that the weapons of our warfare are not carnal but mighty through God to the pulling down of strongholds (2 Corinthians 10:4); helped me focus on the real enemy of my storm and that was Satan himself. It was not my ex-husband; it was demonic encroachment that was out to steal my joy; kill my soul; and destroy my desire to get past this heartache. You see, I had to make an intentional effort to put on the whole armor of God EVERYDAY! I could not take shortcuts in my efforts to stand strong. I could not eliminate the whole armor of God in my efforts to stand strong and I could not rely on myself in my efforts to stand strong. Truthfully, I felt weak and helpless most days. However, I knew that HIS strength was made perfect in my weakness (2 Corinthians 12:9). Despite how I felt, I knew I had to stand strong. I knew I had to fight. I knew my enemy was not a person. I knew the whole armor of God was what I needed to fight successfully and come out victorious. Every piece of armor is significant in this fight. Every piece is used by God to help you stand strong, but you MUST put it on! There comes a time in every believer's walk with God that quoting scriptures is good and knowing scripture is great but walking it out is how we stay strong. Application, application, application! This is where the rubber meets the road as my mom used to say. You either believe God's word or you don't; you either apply it or you don't. It is completely up to you and the decision you make ultimately determines your outcome and ability to stand strong in the fight. The decision you make to follow God in the storm determines your ability to fight and win. If you read the book (the Bible) you will see that we ultimately win the war in the end, but will you stand strong during the battle? Will you conquer your enemy and experience the victory that God has already provided? I declare that YOU WILL WIN but you must fight right! You must fight God's way. You must stand strong on the word and work the word for your benefit. The word is full of promises from God to assist us in the battle that guarantees our win but only if we stand on the promises; only if we stand strong.

When I reflect back to my own personal struggles, I am in awe of one thing and that is my God given strength. I can truly say that I lost my job, mother, marriage and temporarily my ministry but tried to never let anyone see me sweat. Not that I wanted to pretend nothing was going on, but I wanted to display the strength that God was giving me. Did I cry? YES, ALL THE TIME! Did I hurt so bad I thought I would die? YES! But I was constantly reminded that my son was looking at me to see what it looked like for us believers to have the floor kicked out from under us and still stand. It was clear that I was the closest example my son would have on how to survive a storm in life, so I made sure my son never saw me lose control. I made sure my son saw a strong black woman on every front because I wanted him to know that God was in control of my life. I have been a Praise and Worship leader since 2000 and my son has sat in the congregation on numerous occasions and listened to me encourage the saints to hold on and never give up on God. So, who was I to not live out that example before him and show him how awesome God was, keeping his mother when life kicked her in the gut? This is significant because, as a 4-year old girl, I watched my mother weather the storm that I did not even comprehend fully. My father died of a stroke when I was 4 years old; then my brother was killed in the Vietnam war 6 months after my father died; then the house that my mother had worked hard to purchase after my father died caught on fire the week before we were supposed to move in. As an adult I realize the severity of that season for my mother but what I remember is going to two funerals in close proximity to each other and my mother being a tower of strength. I now know that it was only because of her relationship with God. That was my motivation for showing my son how God would keep us in that storm and perform His word over our lives. What I saw in my mother, I wanted to demonstrate to my son and pass down generational strength. It was important to me that I show him rather than tell him. Just as I was able to go back in my memory and use my mother's example of strength in a storm; I wanted my son to have the same reference.

When I went through my battle it seemed like I would never come out or never win. The pain was so unbearable that I thought I was going to die spiritually, emotionally, and physically. As a matter of fact, I would not have been mad at God if He had called me home during that time. However, since God chose to leave me here, I knew it meant I had to fight. I was exhausted from fighting in the natural and trying to figure it out in the natural. When I got tired of trying to work things out on my own, I tapped into the spiritual realm and I let God minister to me. I know that sounds super spiritual but, for me, it is what kept me functioning during this difficult trial. A good question to ask right now is what does tapping into the spiritual realm look like? Great question. For me, it was turning off the television and feeding my spirit only with the things of God. That was the source of my strength. I became strong by strengthening my spirit man and it allowed me to fight the good fight of faith. To the best of my ability I tried to stay tapped into the spirit for strength. Don't get me wrong, I didn't always get it right. I would be telling a lie if I led you to believe I did everything perfectly because I did not. There were some days that I simply failed miserably at being strong and fighting but God's grace and mercy covered me. I had to learn how to quiet my spirit and for me it wasn't easy. I was accustomed to running from sun-up to sun-down and having a life that is full of "stuff". It's difficult to discipline your flesh and spirit to quiet down so that it can get a word from God. However, I was at my wits end and could not breathe from the pain. One thing that I know for sure, when I hit rock bottom, I hit God because He is my foundation.

Reaching rock bottom will teach you quickly how to take God's promises and apply them. I learned how to pray God's scriptures back to Him in total desperation believing that He would come to my rescue. When life requires you to be strong for the battle, it is no longer cute to quote a scripture, it is when you learn to apply the word of God to your very life that provides the strength you need. Then, I noticed that strength came to me when I was able to apply God's word. When I was able to put two and two together, I realized I had the right formula for my life to find the strength that I needed. Applying God's word for me meant studying God's word for scriptures that gave me hope. The hope that I obtained from the scriptures not only made me stronger, but they stopped me from losing control of my tempter and they taught me how to speak life into my situation. So, on many days with tears in my eyes, I would make declarations that my next husband was on the way. With my heart broken into a million pieces, I gained solace in the fact that these light afflictions are not worthy to be compared to the glory which shall be revealed (2 Corinthians 4:17). That gave me hope and strength and allowed me to keep fighting, knowing that God had me; and He totally did. When you go through a storm that requires strength, you really learn to trust God at an entirely different level. You just have to be crazy enough to take God at His word. When the ship is sinking, you must have the blessed assurance that you are going to make it; even if the ship falls apart, you will make it on broken pieces of the ship (Acts 27:27 – Acts 28:5). I knew, somehow and some way, I WAS going to make it. That is the mindset I had to adopt to make sure I didn't quit.

Strength needed for this journey is already inside you. I know, at times, it seems like it is nearly impossible to be strong, but you and God together will get through this. Just BE STRONG because God has something better for you!

STEP 10

Help Others

"But I have prayed for you; that your faith should not fail; and when you are converted, strengthen your brethren." Luke 22:32 (KJV)

I am very clear now, that what we go through is not for us or about us. What we go through are storms meant to strengthen us so that we can help others. I guarantee you that, as you go through your struggles, trials, and difficulties and overcome them; the Lord will send people your way that are traveling through a situation you have already successfully conquered. And, they are looking to you to tell them how you did it. I cannot tell you how many people I have been blessed to help because of my experience and my ability to get to the other side. In the text above Jesus was praying for Peter because Jesus knew the challenges ahead Peter would face, and knew how the Lord would have to humble him in order for Peter to have a ministry after his death that would stand the test of time. The part of Luke 22:32 that I love is, "and when you are converted; strengthen your brethren." God is fully expecting you to pay it forward when you make it out of your storm. This entire concept was foreign to me. I was so grateful to follow God's plan for my path of healing that I was just basking in the healing and living my best life. Living day to day for God and not really thinking about helping others. I was really just existing and not fully understanding the impact my storm or, better yet, my story would have on people.

I was first invited to speak at a Women's Conference by my good friend, Nicolle D. Surratte, proprietor of NspireD by Nicolle (www.nspiredbynicolle.com). I will never forget the topic of my seminar "Overcoming Deadly Emotions". Initially, when she asked me, my first inclination was to say no. I thought it was too soon, I started second guessing my ability to talk about my storm, I even started second guessing my healing but I will always be inspired by the words of my first spiritual father, Bishop S. Todd Townsend, "GO SCARED." So, I accepted the speaking engagement, and I spoke that day. Things went well, but I didn't expect to experience how soul cleansing it would be to talk about my healing process. As I spoke the words that God gave me that day, I remember seeing the light bulbs come on in people's spirits. I saw that the attendees really needed to get over some emotions because they were beginning to understand that negative emotions can really become deadly over time. That day was more of a springboard to me writing this book than anything else so I must say "thank you" to my friend Nicolle for trusting me to be a part of her vision for that day. It became very apparent to me that I had a story to tell. A story that would get women (and men) unstuck. Unstuck from hatred, bitterness, unforgiveness, resentment, grief, doom, and despair. I knew that what I had experienced through divorce was a pain that cut deep. I also knew that healing for me personally, had to be done God's way. Fighting back in the flesh was a thought but it was a fleeting one at best. I was too far along in my walk with God to do it any other way. God and I had a good track record. I had seen God move in my life in amazing ways over the years and I was just crazy enough to trust Him with this part of my life as well.

One thing I did not want to do was drink my sorrows away. I was not at all a drinker. I was raised in a godly home by a pastor, so alcohol was not a part of life for me. However, I had begun to pick up a bottle of wine here and there to try to numb the pain. That lasted for about a month before the spirit of the Lord put a quick end to that. I do not even know what it was exactly, but I knew deep in my spirit that alcohol was not the answer, so God removed that desire from me quickly. I had friends that suggested I see a doctor to get a prescription to help me sleep and focus. I do not like taking pills so that was not an option. Besides, I had heard of too many people becoming addicted to pills and the pills altering their personality and who they were. I had a job that was not conducive to me not bringing my A-game so that was not an option for me either. I did see a therapist once, but when I finished preaching to him the therapist determined I was doing well so I never went to see him again. LOL I'm not knocking therapy as a solution because I feel Christian counseling is a very viable solution and I highly recommend it to those who really need that extra push in the right direction. However, for me, it seemed that God removed all the natural realm healing options from me, and I had no other choice than to do it HIS way.

In prior chapters, you read about my journey to healing; it wasn't a long drawn out story because I made the decision early on to do it God's way and God afforded me the mental fortitude and strength to lean wholly on Him. Because I chose to heal God's way it really did shorten the process to healing for me and I was able to quickly resume a great post-marital friendship with the man that I dated for 5 years and married for 20 years. I had been with him since I was 16 years old and, in my opinion (at that point), he was a very good friend and remains so to this day. I am so very grateful to God and so very blessed that I was able to get through my journey and be completely healed of all deadly emotions. Honestly, it was my tendency to be stubborn (as it relates to not letting anyone think that their exit from my life would leave me in a bad way) that led me to wanting to be healed quickly without any residue. I had seen too many women be angry for years after a painful experience. I had seen too many women become mean, cantankerous, and unkind because of their failure to heal God's way. I was more than determined that would not be my story. I was determined that God's word would come alive in my life. I was determined that I would stand on God's words and God's promise to see me through. I got excited and motivated to search the scriptures for text that would be the shot in the arm I needed to press forward. Ultimately, I wanted my experience to be an example and helpful to others who were experiencing the pains of life.

Chapter 3 gives you a bunch of scriptures that I used to keep me motived and encouraged to heal my heart God's way by standing on God's promises. The list in Chapter 3 is by no means exhaustive so I highly recommend you search God's word for the scriptures that give you hope, motivation and courage to keep fighting God's way. As you might recall, one of my favorites was "better is the end of a thing than the beginning thereof" (Ecclesiastes 7:8 KJV). I was like, "What God? You mean to tell me if I keep going then it is going to get better?" Bet! That's exactly what I did. That scripture was what I hung my hopes and dreams on. I kept going because I believed God enough to know that His word was true. I just had to keep going, keep strapping on my armor of God every day; keep trusting God; keep believing God; keep being obedient to His word; keep going; press forward toward the mark. Before I knew it, I was on the other side of the storm. Admittedly, I only made it because God kept me. To this day, every time I hear "God Blocked It" by Kurt Carr, the tears just roll down my face. That song is confirmation to me that God blocked every suicidal attempt, every attempt the enemy made on my life to get me addicted to alcohol and sleeping pills, every attempt to get me to be an angry black woman, but GOD BLOCKED IT! Tears of joy, gratitude and thankfulness that God blocked every attempt of the enemy to destroy me during this storm. The first verse of this song says:

The devil had a plan to kill me I know, but God intercepted his plan and told the devil no. God blocked it; He wouldn't let it be so.

When I think about every attempt the devil made on my life to wipe me out and how God blocked it, I just weep because I am extremely grateful. That is why I praise God the way I do. That is why my hallelujah is as loud as it is. That is why I dance. That is why I shout. God blocked it and would not let it be so. I am here to tell you that, if that don't get your fire started, then your wood is wet!

So, shortly after I spoke at my friend Nicolle's conference, I began to have women come up to me at the conference and at church to tell me that their story is similar to mine but they were still stuck. It was then that I knew, for me personally, my story; my trial; my storm was going to be used by God to

HELP OTHERS! Initially, I just thought God brought me though the storm because He promised He would, and I would just live my life healed and whole. What I didn't know was that He would use my story to HELP OTHERS! Helping others was so very organic for me and I must say that I take no credit for that whatsoever. Growing up, God placed me in an environment where helping others was the theme of the day. My mother would bring homeless people to our Thanksgiving dinner table every year, then allow them to bathe in our bathroom and send them on their way with full stomachs and clean clothes. Thinking back on it, it had to be the hand of God on my mother's life bringing complete strangers in her home to be around her children, in a world where most people do not trust strangers. Not only are strangers rarely trusted but, the thought of bringing them into your home around your children would not be a consideration for most. But God had His hand on my mother for sure. She was a single mother raising five children on one income; however, she always had an open hand and heart to help others. This is the generational blessing that my mother passed to her children, HELP OTHERS!

It is God that allows me to cross paths with women who need to hear that God brought me through so that they can have the blessed assurance that He will bring them through as well. Why? Because if He did it for me, then He will do it for you. The question is will you allow God to use you to help others? Of course, we all want to be helped out of our situation but then we must pay it forward. We must help bring others out of their pain by speaking the word of God into their situation for them when they can't; keeping them accountable to pray and do it God's way; being a listening ear; being their voice of reason or just being there.

Everyone wants the hurting to stop and we all want to be over the storm and completely healed. But, the truth of the matter is some of us get stuck and are still stuck today, completely unaware, because we want to heal *our way* not realizing:

- Our way is demonic.

- Our way is fleshly and takes years, even decades.
- Our way can sometimes land us in jail.
- Our way can be embarrassing.
- Our way can drive others out of our lives.
- Our way makes it difficult for others to love us.
- Our way keeps us angry and bitter.
- Our way leaves us without meaningful friendship.

So, let me HELP YOU! Our way is not the way. We can only effectively heal God's way. Using His words, His strength, His wisdom, and His way to get through the storms of life. His way means we crucify our flesh. His way means we get into His word and learn how we are to behave, how we are to speak, and how we are to respond to the storm. How we are to fight. His way means we don't engage in arguments with people whom the enemy sends our way (remember never argue with a fool).

One day during my healing process I remember being so angry at my ex-husband. I remember being filled with rage. In that moment, the enemy reared his ugly head. Even though I was praying diligently and believing God for my healing, I had a real human moment and I just wanted to lash out with revenge. I felt that what the enemy had told me to do was justified. After all, if I had done it, no one would have blamed me. But in the words of Helen Baylor, "I had a praying mother." All I could hear in my spirit was my mother saying, "vengeance is mine; I will repay, saith the Lord (Romans 12:19)." As I said earlier, I was raised by a pastor. My mother used everyday life situations and circumstances to teach us scripture and millions of times in our lives, my siblings and I would hear my mother say, "Vengeance is mine." She not only quoted it to us, but she lived it in front of us. So that was pretty much the end of me not being aware of the enemy's attempts to "back door me" as my Bishop John Edmondson says. The enemy will sneak up from behind and try to slip into your spirit. If you are not careful and prayed up, you will have a very "dumb day" as Bishop John says. It is times like that day when I am thankful for being raised by a praying mother who was a walking Bible. She taught us the word and taught us to pray at a very young age. It was her lifestyle of worship and her lifestyle of teaching me the word that saved me that day because God used her voice to remind me, "I got this my daughter." Well needless to say, I did not lash out at my ex-husband and, as a result, we have such a great post-divorce friendship. I am thankful because who has time to hate? Not me. I want to be an extension of God's love in the earth not quote His word then treat people mean and be hateful towards them. I am just not interested in being a mean person. I want to be God's light in the earth. God is light and in Him is no darkness at all (1 John 1:5 KJV).

So, my goal, my life mission is to help other women (and men) heal life's hurts God's way. There really is no other option. Even if you try your own way for a while, you will ultimately fail because God's way is the only way. The statements below were my motivation to crucify my flesh and do it God's way which, helped me help others:

1. Ultimately, I want God to be pleased with me. I wanted to make Him a proud Father. Growing up without a father (mine died when I was four), I found the love of God to be so validating especially after I tried to fill God's space with ungodly things as a promiscuous teenager. Discovering that God loved me like a Father was so liberating to me. I have spent my days wanting to make Him proud. I wanted God to brag on me. Not that I have always gotten it right because I have not. I mostly got it wrong but thank God for His grace.

2. I did not want my healing to take a decade. I said this earlier but there was an older woman whom I love dearly and greatly respect who told me, "If I had forgiven my ex-husband as quickly as you forgave yours I wouldn't be on all this medicine I'm on." I wanted to heal quickly because I knew I wasn't meant to be single, therefore I wanted to heal and go into my next marriage completely whole with no baggage.

3. I did not want to sow any bad seeds. Galatians 6:7 KJV says "be not deceived; God is not mocked: for whatsoever a man soweth that shall he also reap." From a child until now, one thing I hated was being in trouble with a parent. I hated being in trouble with my mom. I did not want to get any whippings because Rev. Gladys Durham did not play games with us. One thing I know for sure, when you sow crazy seeds, that is what you reap. I knew enough about God's word to know that I could not afford to sow bad seeds. I did my best to sow good seeds because I wanted to reap a good harvest. I knew that, during this process, I had to sow good seeds. I did not always want to, and I had to die to my flesh daily because in this flesh dwelleth no good thing. I did my best to sow good seeds. The great thing about beating your flesh under subjection to allow yourself to sow good seeds is, when you begin to reap the good harvest, it becomes easier to continue sowing good seeds. Keep striving for

righteousness because I promise it will pay off in the end, just trust me.

All these reasons contributed to my ability to help others today. Helping others is what we are called to do. This entire process of healing my hurt God's way birthed purpose in me. What has become increasingly clear is, this trial birthed my purpose to help others heal God's way. It is the good works Paul wrote of in Ephesians 2:10 (KJV), "For we are his workmanship, created in Christ Jesus unto good works, which God hath before ordained that we should walk in them." My purpose is clear, and God ordained.

I plan to spend the rest of my days helping others walk through *Healing Life's Hurts* God's way through these ten steps. In this new season, as I walked in my purpose, I began to understand the "why" behind the hurt. God used me to walk through these steps so that He could birth this purpose in me. God could not and would not use me until I was healed fully and no longer walking in offense. Be encouraged to go through your process because God will use your victory over your trial and hurt to help others but only after you have healed your hurt God's way.

Blessings!!!!

CONCLUSION

My purpose for writing this book is solely to get people unstuck. Sometimes the vicissitudes of life have a way of catching us off guard. Sometimes the trials of life knock us down. Sometimes trouble seems to kick us right in the gut and take our breath away right when we least expect it. If we are not careful, we will get stuck in the storm because we do not know how to move forward. Pain can be paralyzing. I get it, even though I write about the steps I took to heal, it was not a pretty picture or a nice neat journey. It was not wrapped up a pretty package with a bow. I struggled just like everyone else to get my life together after life happened to me. Do not think that this book is about being perfect and getting it right all the time, it isn't. It is about getting yourself healed so you can avoid living life as a bitter person. This story was my journey and how I did it successfully. Everyone handles storms differently, but these are tools I know will get you unstuck if you work them.

My desire is that the tools I provided here will get you healed from the inside out so you can live your life as God intended and not live beneath your privilege.

Storms can come upon us quickly and we often find ourselves unprepared. If you are going through a storm, then I pray this book helps you navigate through successfully. If you are not in a storm, then I pray this book gets you ready. The best way to handle a storm is to be ready for it. This is a book designed to help you heal your life's hurt but do it God's way. Some of us were not raised in the church nor have scriptures imbedded in our spirits that provide the fortitude we need to see us through a rough patch. Some of us are not surrounded by people who can guide us through the pain of a storm. Some of us don't know that Jesus is in the boat with us riding through the storm. The interesting thing about trials, storms, difficulties and heartache is that it happens to everyone at some point in our lives. We don't usually get to say when it happens or how it happens; it just sometimes happens and seemingly comes out of nowhere.

This book was written to guide you back to wholeness; back to a healed heart; back to the place in God where you can keep walking and growing and living out your purpose. Please know that even in the midst of your storm, God will not put more on you than you can bear. It might not feel like it but, if you find yourself in a storm, then trust and believe that He will bring you through the storm.

God gave me this revelation and I pray it blesses you the way it blessed me. It is often said when life hands you lemons make lemonade. Well, everything you need to turn the lemons (heartache, pains, storms, troubles) into lemonade can be found right in the word of God.

- Lemons (the storms of life)

- Water (John 4:13-14) NKJV "Jesus answered and said to her, "whoever drinks of this water will thirst again, but whoever drinks of the water that I shall give him will never thirst. But the water that I shall give him will become in him a fountain of water springing up into everlasting life"; (Ephesians 5:26) KJV "that he might sanctify and cleanse it with the washing of the water by the word." The WORD is the WATER!

- Honey (Psalm 19:10b) "sweeter also than honey on the honeycomb." God's precepts and statues that we follow is the HONEY, sweetener!

Essentially when life hands you lemons, you must make spiritual, holy ghost filled lemonade by adding the water of the Word and the honey sweetness of God's law, testimony, statutes, commandment and judgement. Mix that all together and enjoy the refreshment that God provides by our obedience in Him. AMEN!

I struggled writing this book because I really felt like there are enough self-help books out there with enough biblical counsel so I didn't feel my book would make a difference. I had to go back and read Chapter 5 of my own book to encourage myself like King David did. If this book helps just one person then I know it was not in vain. I speak life into this body of work that it will be successful and bless the masses; I speak life to your very soul. I agree with you for whatever situation you find yourself in that you will use the words of this book to work your way back to healing. Healing is the children's bread and God's promise to us.

I'm thankful that God gave me the strength and fortitude to get through my trial so that I could use my testimony to bless others. I didn't want this book to be about what my ex-husband did or make him out to be a bad person because truthfully he was hurting as badly as I was and well you know how the saying goes; "hurt people hurt people". Besides, focusing on him and what I felt he had done to me would have been a distraction in getting me to the place of my healing. Doing so would have had me focusing on the fruit of the issue and not the root of the issue. The root of the issue was the underlying pain I felt. I needed to dig down inside myself and do the healing work required to get me to wholeness. The fruit was rehearsing what was done to me over and over and over again. This was fruit that needed to die, and it would only die and never return if the root was destroyed. Focusing on the root of the issue (the real underlying problem) is the only way to heal and not visit the situation again, take the test again, or have more bad fruit grow. I pray you can dig down to the root of your pain and pluck it out and eliminate bad fruit from growing and attaching itself to your spirit. I remember getting my first house and had a small planter bed in the front yard. I grew up in the city, the urban concrete jungle. My mother worked her fingers to the bone to provide for 9 children so there was no lesson on gardening, growing up. When I started trying to garden, I was so excited to plant flowers and plants in my little garden. After about two years I noticed that weeds started growing up. I would pull them, and they would return. One day I was fussing and complaining about weeds, so my next-door neighbor came over and showed me how to pull a weed from the root so that the root was removed. Once the root was removed, that weed had no choice but to leave and never return because it had nothing holding it up under the surface to allow it to grow back. That is exactly how we must focus on our issues. Don't be afraid to dig deep down into the root of your issue so you can pull it up to stop the bad fruit from growing. If you fail to do so, then your bad fruit or weeds will continue to grow and make it nearly impossible for you to heal. Hebrews 12:15 NIV says, "See to it that no one falls short of the grace of God; and that **no bitter root grows up to cause trouble and defile many**." As a result of this revelation, this book became about getting people to a place where they are really ready to start the process of healing God's way. This is not about rehearing wrongs that were done to you. If you are at a place where you can't stop rehearsing the wrong done to you then you are not ready to move forward toward healing. You literally have to do as the Apostle Paul said in Philippians 3:13b-14 (KJV) "forgetting those things which are behind and reaching forth unto those things which are before. I press toward the mark for the prize of the high calling of God in Christ Jesus." We must press forward. Rehearsing wrongs is what gets us stuck. That is where the enemy tries to keep us, but the devil is a liar. I do declare that you will get unstuck today and you will press forward toward the mark. That you will not build a concrete foundation where you were only meant to pitch a tent. You will get free from focusing on the things that destroy your soul and you will move forward to take steps toward healing your hurt God's way. I thank God for all the spiritual fathers and mothers and sisters and brothers and elders that He surrounded me with and refused to let me stay stuck. If you are stuck, I pray the pages of this book get you to where you need to be to begin your journey to healing God's way. God is faithful and loving and kind and true and His desire is that you are whole, healthy and healed. Allow this book to be your roadmap to a journey of wholeness and complete healing.

I will tell you that my story is far from over, but I thank God that He got me through my journey of healing. One that took me from a broken marriage, a broken heart, and broken dreams to a life of happiness. A life filled with an amazing husband, Darius B. Nelson, an awesome church, Victory In Christ Christian Center, an amazing job at BET Investments, a loving son, Ernest Hickerson and awesome family and friends both far and wide. I am truly blessed but it's all because God gave me the grace to go through the ten steps to healing God's way.

CLOSING PRAYER

Father God, in the name of Jesus, I pray for the person who has read this book. I pray, God, that whatever state they find themselves in on their road to healing and wholeness You would walk with them. Father You said the steps of a good man are ordered by You so I pray You break their will and give them the strength, courage, faith, wisdom, and tenacity to follow Your lead. God be a lamp to their feet and a light to their path. Father show yourself mighty and strong on their behalf. Do those things that seem impossible to man but are possible only through you. You are God who is able to do exceedingly and abundantly above so I pray that whatever is being faced by this reader that You heavenly Father would sustain them. God You are our refuge and our strength, and You are a very present help so we call on Your name Father that You would be a PRESENT HELP! We call on Your name and we make our requests known to You because Your word says before we call You answer and while we are yet speaking You hear. So, hear our prayer Oh God and incline Your ear to our petitions right now in the name of Jesus. I pray God that You allow the reader to confront the issues and demons that need to be confronted and You allow the reader to slay every demon in Jesus' name. God we pull down every stronghold and every high place in the reader's life that would attempt to exalt itself against the knowledge of You and bring every thought that is not like You and teach it to obey You. God, we know that You are the great physician and that You are able to heal, deliver and set free. I thank You God that by the stripes of Jesus the reader is healed today. They will no longer be held captive by the pain and hurt and fear that paralyzed them in the past, but they will walk bold in You and in their healing in Jesus' name. I decree and declare that their healing journey will be expeditious because of their obedience to Your word. I pray that You heal hurting hearts and I intercede for them right now that you put the pieces of their heart back together. Father restore them right now. God restore the years the cankerworm stole and just as You did Job, bless them abundantly more. Then God I pray You hide them in the cleft of the rock and keep them safe while they go through this healing process. Father I thank You that Your name is a strong tower and we are able to run to it for safety. I decree and declare safety. To the woman who was married and is now living alone, I pray safety, I declare all fear of harm be gone right now in the name of Jesus. Angels mount up and protect your daughter and her children if there be any. For the man who has lost hope and is feeling lonely, I pray that You cause him to run to You to restore his hope in all that was lost. I pray for the broken and discouraged. Father we may be troubled on every side but we are not distressed; we may be perplexed but we are not in despair; we may be persecuted but YOU have never forsaken us; we may be cast down but we are not destroyed. You have taught our fingers to fight and our hands to war so Father help us strap up daily with the full armor of

God so we can fight effectively in the spirit and win through the blood of Jesus Christ. Father we have been young yet now are we old; but we have NEVER seen the righteous forsaken nor His seed begging bread. So, Father meet every need of Your sons and daughters who are holding this book in their hands. Make a way out of no way. You promised to supply our needs according to Your riches in glory, so Father SHOW OFF on their behalf. Let them know You are right by their side because You promised never to leave nor forsake them. Let them feel Your peace that surpasses all understanding. Give them peace that the world can't take away.

Now Father help us to trust in you with all our hearts and not lean unto our own understanding. God in all of our ways we ACKNOWLEDGE You; we ACKNOWLEDGE You; we ACKNOWLEDGE You. You are our source; You are our shield; You are our banner; You are our protection; You are our high tower; You are our exceeding great reward; You are our sustainer and giver of life. Everything we need is in Your hands so Father we surrender our will to Yours. Have Your way in our lives and lead, guide and direct us however You see fit. You are the potter and we are clay. Shape us and mold us in this season into whatever you want us to be. We are open; we are ready, and we are yielded so Holy Spirit have Your way in our lives. We decrease so You can increase in every area of our lives. We give you free reign over our will and emotions in Jesus' name! So, Father to You be all gory, all honor and all praise in Jesus' name, AMEN!

Made in the USA
Middletown, DE
07 July 2020